The Meaning of It All in Everyday Speech

SCM PRESS

For Hugh, Liz, Henry
and Alexandra

0 334 02786 1

First published 1999
by SCM Press
9–17 St Albans Place, London N1 0NX

SCM Press is a division of
SCM-Canterbury Press Ltd

Typeset by Regent Typesetting, London
and printed in Great Britain by
Biddles Ltd, Guildford and King's Lynn

Contents

The Meaning of It All in Everyday Speech

Introduction

the strange and little-known world of
ordinary language

This book is another expedition into the strange and little-known world of ordinary language. Its predecessor was about the word **life:**[1] this book is about **it**, and again we are trying to discover what vision of the world and of the human condition is ours and belongs to us all, because it is built into our common language.

I've been led to devise this new method of religious enquiry by three main considerations. First, during the last two decades of the twentieth century the culture as a whole, and education in particular, have come to be more and more dominated by science and technology. The relative position of philosophy and theology – the two subjects I have cared most about – has come to look weaker and weaker. As topics like language, consciousness, cosmology and time get taken over by science, philosophy is left looking relatively amateurish, dispossessed, fretful and increasingly redundant. As for theology, it is disabled by its own lack of an agreed and fruitful method. All forms of religious belief in modern society appear to be an intellectual mess, self-indulgent and non-rational, and theology has so far found no effective research method of its own. It knows only the method of critical history, which doesn't deliver religious truth. But it clings to history, and it has no policy for clearing up the mess that it is in and at last putting religious belief and life on a tolerably rational basis.

It is not surprising that people wonder how much longer philosophy and theology can survive as literary genres and academic disciplines. How can they defend themselves when it seems that, unlike science and technology, they are not actually discovering and delivering anything useful to people?

Secondly, while I was thinking of these things I recalled Wittgenstein's teaching about the priority of ordinary language. We are always in ordinary language first of all, and it has already given us a basic common world-view, which science, for example, always presupposes. But Wittgenstein did not spell out in detail what this common world-view is.[2] Is it an historical product? Could we spell it out in detail, and perhaps one day learn to write its history?

The third consideration to be mentioned is the fact that for many years I have been noticing how rich our language is in idioms and proverbs of great philosophical and religious interest. I have got into the habit of including some of them in my books, because they make philosophical points with great economy and clarity.

As I have reported elsewhere, I began a few years ago to collect the most interesting of these idioms, at first with the thought of using them to persuade a sceptical public that they are already talking philosophy when they say things like 'I couldn't believe my eyes!' I had an idea of writing the common philosophy of life of the English-speaking peoples, but as the collection of idioms grew I was increasingly attracted, first to the word 'life', and then later to the word 'it'.

In retrospect it is extraordinary that when I began these enquiries I had no idea of the conclusions to which I would be led. Not to spoil the fun, I will say no more here than that **life** turned out to be very young, whereas **it** is very old. **Life**, in the very rich and religiously-weighty sense it now has in ordinary language, has developed only in the last 150 years or so, and has been taken into ordinary language in a big way only since about 1950. **It**, by contrast, is very ancient. Many of the it-idioms associate **it** with phrases and terms such as the Inevitable, Fate, Destiny, what must be, the Will of God, It-all, the gods, Everything and so on, conjuring up the idea of a vast uncomprehended and inexorable backdrop to human life that somehow we must come to terms with. We must **face up to it** and

accept it, because **it can't be helped.** As the Bible says about God, **There's no getting away from it.**

The it-idioms are much more numerous than the life-idioms, of which I found only about 150, nearly all of them rather new. At first I expected that the prominence of it-idioms in modern English would turn out to be post-1660, having to do with the growing influence of the third-person descriptive language of science. I thought also that the restoration of the tragic sense of life by writers such as Schopenhauer, Hardy and Conrad would turn out to have helped make us into people who have adopted a host of it-idioms into our everyday speech. But two days with dictionaries showed me that many it-idioms go all the way back to the beginnings of the English language. English-speakers were never pure theists: their idioms were always rather eclectic, speaking of life's backdrop in terms that mingled reference to God, Fate, causal necessity, Luck and plain old **It.** We were always mongrels in our language and beliefs, as in our genes; and we still are. All that one can say with confidence is that in the past century or so the it-idioms have become more numerous and suggestive. I *mean* 'suggestive', because many it-idioms have associations scatological, sexual, fearsome and sublime, as well as religious; and all these associations are interestingly interconnected.

Again, this is an essay in 'democratic philosophy'. The method is empirical: I'm not trying to prove *my* views, and persuade *you* to adopt them. I'm trying to find out what our language gives us all to believe. Once I had become sufficiently sensitized to the word **it,** I found the it-idioms utterly transporting; and I would like above all else to be able to communicate that excitement. There is a world-view of ordinariness, but it is almost unknown, and as we unravel it we are startled to recognize that something so strange and exciting is also so intimately familiar to us.

Since **it** is very old, going far back into pre-Christian times, and **life** is relatively very new, the difficult question arises of how in modern ordinariness they fit together. Sometimes they overlap and even coincide: **How's life?** and **How's it going?,**

How is it with you?, and **How are things with you?** are inter-changeable. Otherwise, do we ordinarily see **it** as part of **life**, or do we see **it** as **life**'s Other and contrasting backdrop? If the latter, which of them is now the religious object? These are deep and interesting matters which, so far as I know, nobody has thought of investigating. Ordinariness is a strange world that we have as yet scarcely begun to explore.

From all this you will gather that I am suggesting that in a period when many people are understandably sceptical about the utility and the prospects of both philosophy and theology, we might give both subjects a shot in the arm by investigating ordinariness. In the past, both philosophy and theology were élite subjects. Their future now depends upon whether they can democratize themselves. To do that, they need to investigate the metaphysics of ordinariness, its understanding of the human condition and its religious and moral valuations. We need to stop telling people what the religious authorities think they ought to believe, and instead start to show people what they already *do* believe.

The huge advantage of investigating ordinariness, and doing so by studying idioms in our common language, turns out to be that we begin to discover a very large area of neglected (and, admittedly, somewhat untidy) common ground. It has been a cliché that in matters of faith, philosophy and values modern societies are extremely pluralistic. The popular metaphor pictures society as a religious, philosophical and moral super-market, with thousands of different brightly-packaged products clamouring for our attention, and with the confused shoppers snatching items and filling their trolleys with a bit of this and a bit of that. But the study of ordinary language opens up a completely different picture, by revealing to us what a lot we all of us share, and how interesting it is.

I am suggesting that if philosophy and theology were to pay more attention to the unknown, unrecognized world-view of ordinariness, studying it descriptively and taking their agenda from it, they might give themselves a new lease of life. They would at last convincingly democratize themselves, and their work would be of great interest to the public and to those who need to communicate with the public.

In antiquity there was a motto: *gnōthi seauton*, know thyself; and there was a very long tradition that equated self-knowledge with religious knowledge – theology, the knowledge of God. We can now give a clear meaning to these ancient ideas. By investigating the philosophy of life, the world-view and the religious outlook that is embedded in our ordinary language, we are finding out for the first time who we are and what we really believe – and we are at last beginning to put religious thought on something like a rational footing.

In this book I follow the same rule as was used in the life-book. The major idioms to which I'm drawing attention are printed in **bold roman** type, while *italics* are used for related and relevant idioms and popular quotations. It has turned out to be more difficult than **Life** was. Material is harder to collect, and the history much harder to reconstruct. Again I will welcome ideas and suggestions, and again promise to try to incorporate them in any future second edition that may be called for.

Because of the queer novelty *and* familiarity of these ideas I hope you will accept in this book a rather spiralling method of writing, which keeps me returning to some themes and treating them again in more detail. We are seeking understanding in an area where systematic order and clarity are not to be found, and we are attempting something quite new.

Be warned that you will soon learn what I have had to learn: that ordinary language is astonishingly dense and complex. To understand a simple idiom you may have to wade through five or six layers of symbolic extension and transformation of the original root meanings. In fact, ordinary language turns out to be more demanding than Heidegger and Hegel rolled into one. If you doubt me, just analyse and explain the following three it-idioms, which all 'mean' the same – that *I'm done for*:

It's all up with me
I've had it
It's all over

In Britain, ordinariness likes to present itself as being plain-spoken and straightforward. In fact, it is fiendishly complex and carries a huge amount of concealed baggage. One begins to understand why it is so neglected. But it is *ourselves*: to understand it would perhaps be to understand the real human genome.

Steven Shakespeare and Hugh Rayment-Pickard have kindly read the manuscript and made helpful criticisms, some of which I have accepted. On two points, though, I have proved obstinate. The twenty-eight sections still stand in the sequence in which they were written, showing the rather unsystematic way in which one has to explore new territory. And I have resisted the argument that 'your case is best made by those idioms where it is unlikely to be functioning as a defined pronoun'. I still persist in thinking that even where it is something very specific, it can still very often be felt to present a threat to personal relations, leading us to try to **make light of it, play it down,** and say **Don't mention it,** or **Say no more about it,** or **Not a bit of it.** I'm interested in the way ordinary language pictures us as *surrounded* by an 'it' that we must try to fend off.

And thanks again to Linda Allen for word-processing.

Emmanuel College, July 1999.   D.C.

. . . there ought to be a book about it

People often say that **there ought to be a book about it,** but nobody has yet ventured to write such a book. No doubt they hesitate to **face up to it** because **it** hints at something whose precise identity is being withheld. **It** comes out of the unknown like *ET*, which is not only short for 'extra-terrestrial' but also sounds as if it might be a variant of, or a nickname for **it**. It provokes and intrigues us because it is a neuter, provisional subject about which we may or may not become better informed as the sentence unfolds. We don't know yet whether **it** may not turn out to be something supernatural, or a monster, alien and perhaps unclean, like **The Thing** (1951, remade 1982), which was the first-ever space monster on film.[3] When people say '**that thing!**' they express the force of their revulsion precisely by being inexplicit, and in the same way writers and film makers understand that to create the strongest effects of dread and horror they must **keep it dark**, associating **it** with the unknown and the mysterious (and thereby perhaps also linking **it** to IT, information technology). **It** has always been close both to the Unconscious, the **Id**, and to children, who love stories about how seemingly-fearsome monsters can be befriended and tamed by them in secret. In E. Nesbit's *Five Children and It* (1902), as in *ET*, the children instinctively understand that it would be best not to try to tell adults about their own private monster and their dealings with him, or it. **It's serious, it's no joke,** for **it** – together with related terms such as *the Thing*, **that thing**, **the Alien** and **the Other** – has the power to evoke something nameless, unspecific and unthinkable that confronts us and surrounds us: the archaic religious object. Interestingly and curiously, in children's games 'it' is the one who must catch the others, the one whom you must keep away from, the one who is taboo. His touch contaminates, for when he catches you, you yourself immediately become **it**.

It is not at all surprising that writers have hesitated to **get on with it** and **put it down in black and white**.[4] But **here it is** at last: now you can **read all about it**.

2

It does not stand for anything

Unlike most other words, it does not have a meaning. It does not stand for anything. It is nothing more than the third person singular neuter pronoun, once spelt 'hit'. The dictionary cannot do more than describe its grammatical status and the wide range of jobs that it is used to do. Illustrating its uses, the dictionary also draws attention to its gathering of varied metaphorical associations and its emotional force. All this is what makes it so religious, unsettling in its emptiness and its peculiar evocative power. It is everywhere in the language, doing the strangest things. And in fact this present book will show that just in the varied uses of the little word it we can find the whole syllabus of religious thought. We may even find the beginnings of a modern theology in the relation between It and Life.

If you are a person who searches for God, you must already know that God is no longer to be found in the objective world, and God is no longer to be found in the supposed 'depths' of human psychology. God is not out there in or beyond outer space, and God is not inside us in inner space. Nobody nowadays purports to infer the existence of God from facts about the world, and nobody now really thinks that 'the mind' is an empty room inside our skulls in which spirit-beings may take up residence, 'indwelling' or 'possessing' us. There is only one sphere remaining in which religious enquiry can profitably be conducted, and that is the world of *language*, which is by a very long way the greatest and strangest world of all. People say that the search for God is a search for meaning; but as meaning, like truth, is found only in language, it should be obvious to us all by now that the religious object cannot be looked for anywhere else but in language. It is curious that the religious object should reveal itself in the strange behaviour of some of the commonest and least regarded words in the language; and curiouser still that the search for meaning should lead us to look at a word – a joker word, a jack-of-all-trades word – that doesn't actually *have* a meaning of its own.

3

Sacred Letters

Traditional synonyms for theology: – the study of *scripture*, writings; *Sacred Letters*, the study of the Word in which everything that is made has been made.

The scriptural faiths have understood that the only way to religious truth is by the study of *language*. Why have we forgotten it?

We British seem almost actively to dislike language. Certainly we find it very difficult to accept that we inhabit our own language: that it is the world we live in and the air we breathe. So far as we think about these things at all, we think that our own language is nature, invisible and transparent like the air, and that in all normal circumstances it can therefore be disregarded. Persons well-endowed with British 'common sense' regard all attempts to persuade them otherwise as 'mere semantics', an expression I often hear being used against me! To double the irony, people regularly quote Stephen Hawking's remarks in *A Brief History of Time* about the triviality of a linguistic approach to philosophy – the multiple irony being that they wouldn't be quoting Hawking as an authority if he did not in his own person show so eloquently what it is for language to be all we have – and maybe, almost all we need – for our effective functioning as human beings. If you are paralysed but in language you can do almost anything; whereas if you are able-bodied but not in language you can do nothing.

We are always in language. Our language shapes everything we can do, or perceive, or think, or believe. When we examine the deep philosophical and religious feelings and assumptions, built into ordinary language, that shape the way we in turn build the world of everyday life, we begin to see that philosophy and theology might yet become descriptive subjects. They teach us truths that we already know, but are unaware of because they are so close and familiar.

The religion that is hidden in ordinariness is discoverable simply by paying attention to words. It is truly ecumenical: it is what everyone believes. But it is of course *not* historically unchanging, as many of the 'positive' religious systems claim to be. Slowly, it develops; and we happen to live in a period when ordinary language and the ordinary-life-world are changing relatively more rapidly than usual. Interesting times.

4

Religious immanence

The twentieth century just ending has been the century of the Death of God. Hardly anybody still defends the old scholastic metaphysics of God, except for reasons of obedience, loyalty and tradition. To judge by their own language, which is all we have to go by, most conservative believers are now content to make do with a simple anthropomorphic notion of God as a very great and powerful, but friendly, invisible quasi-human person. Others use language which suggests that god-talk poeticizes the belief that love is the highest value, by saying something to the effect that 'God is a force for love that is at the heart of the Universe', while also insisting that what they say must be understood not mythologically but realistically. (Where and what 'the heart of the Universe' is, we are not told.) But for most people, and for Western culture as a whole, the old realistic metaphysics is dead and the old theocentric piety no longer latches on to anything that transcends this world. It is now expressive rather than descriptive; it stops in the here and now. It no longer carries us up to anything Above us, nor carries us forward to anything yet to come.

The consequence of this is that the relation to God has been brought down into the present moment and this world. The relation to God, in religious existentialism, is demythologized into the relation to one's own existence, to which one must commit oneself as unconditionally as one used to be committed to God. The relation to God, in Heidegger's philosophy, is demythologized into the relation to Being, now understood to be simply pure Empty transience, the passing show of all things.[5] The whole world of experience has become as light for us as it is for East Asian Buddhists – and many of us do not find the lightness of Being at all 'unbearable'. Certainly we can and we do nowadays give our unconditional love to things that we know are transient all through and will soon pass away for ever. And thirdly, as I have argued elsewhere, during the past few decades in ordinary language the relation to God has been demythologized into a religious attitude to life, just *life*, the process of things in the human life-world, which we now love, think sacred and commit ourselves to, as if *our life itself* has become the new religious object.[6]

Thus the religious object may nowadays be spoken of as love, as 'existence', as Being and as life. The old central authorities that used to police religious language have largely broken down, and as a result both the old religious vocabulary and the old religious attitudes have become 'disseminated': that is, they have been extended metaphorically and they have been splashed over a great variety of this-worldly objects.[7] Think, for example, of the great variety of things and persons that during the 1990s have come to be described as 'icons'. It is this wide scattering of religious language over a great variety of objects that has made the old narrow orthodoxies seem so irrelevant and powerless.

As a result of the dissemination, then, our language now incorporates a surprising amount of displaced god-talk. As well as the investment with religious value of the words *existence, being* and *life*, already mentioned, a number of periphrases for God (doubtless originally reverential) are still heard: *the Good Lord, the Almighty, the Supreme Being*, and *One Above*. There are others with a precautionary and even mockingly-ironical flavour. We might once have used such terms so as not to risk being overheard by God in the act of taking his Name in vain. These terms include *Providence, Fate, Somebody Up There* and perhaps also **It had to be** and **But it was not to be**, together with *Fortune, Luck* and *the lap of the gods*. The old habit of leaving things for God to know and judge is displaced onto *Time* and *History* in such expressions as 'truth will out', 'time will tell' and 'history will judge'.

A particularly interesting group of expressions is the group that we are presently concerned with. I have already hinted that we should divide them into two sets. The singular expressions **It, The Thing, that thing,** the **Other,** the **Alien,** the **strange** and the **Unknown** are apt to conjure up strong and specific emotions of horror, dread, supernatural terror and even perhaps disgust. These are very archaic religious emotions. By contrast, the more general, plural and even 'cosmic' expressions, such as **It All, Things** and **Everything** evoke in a somewhat cooler way the whole of a person's situation and prospects, considered from a finalizing point of view and as they bear upon her overall well-being.

In this second area, when we **ask after** somebody's general well-being we may phrase our enquiry, **How are things with you?, How's it all going?** Or, **Is everything all right?** And we may get such replies as **Things are fine, thanks, It's all going very well** or, less cheerfully, **Not too good: everything's gone pear-shaped lately.** Until not very long ago such a general enquiry about another person's overall health and well-being might well have been understood to be a *religious* enquiry, meaning roughly: **How are things in general going for you:** *how is God treating you?* I can remember sometimes hearing people say in response to this type of enquiry things such as *Not too bad at present, thank God,* or *God's been good to me.* But nowadays the same 'cosmic' enquiry about how you personally are coping with your own circumstances and the way things in general are bearing upon you is more likely to be seen as a psychological enquiry. Some people are strong, resilient and in good spirits, but others **find it hard to cope with,** and others again succumb to anxiety, perhaps, or depression or both. People's individual ups and downs used to be interpreted theologically, but nowadays are much more likely to be interpreted psychologically. In both dispensations, however, the ups and downs have a 'cosmic' quality, for in both cases we are asking **How do you feel about things?** Or perhaps – wonderful idiom – **How is it with you?** We are asking about somebody's global attitude, or their feelings about life-as-a-whole. And in our psychologically-minded age the global or overall attitude still has a religious flavour. It is still *bliss* to be on a roll, and *hell* to be stuck in depression.

So far then, I have proposed a rough distinction between **It, The Thing, That Thing** and similar expressions used to evoke a notion of some particular thing that is unspecified, veiled as yet and intriguing, but perhaps fearsome or inexorable or even disgusting; and on the other hand **It All, Things** and **Everything**, more general expressions that conjure up the way the whole of things is for a person.

There is a complication, though, in that the word **it** can be used in both ways: both to refer to a particular as yet unknown, and also to evoke the whole of things. Thus **How is it with you?** expresses a general query, just as **Take it easy** is often used interchangeably with **Take things easy**. Indeed, it will soon become clear that **it,** by being empty of meaning, is almost limitlessly evocative. Precisely because **it** has no specific meaning and is in **itself** as neutral and neuter as can be, it turns out in its range of uses to be more weirdly powerful and evocative than almost any other word in the language.

Bear in mind in what follows the hypothesis that **it** is a sort of Joker, a non-realist religious word with the power to give us a sudden *frisson* or shiver of wonder and dread. **It** suddenly opens a crack in the world. **It knocks you sideways.**

5

The *unmentionable*, the *unspeakable*

The fact that **it**, in **itself**, is neuter and has no gender of its own makes it peculiarly emotionally ambivalent. **It** may be anything ungendered with which we have to do. How are we to react to **it**? It may be with disgust, or fascination, or terror, or anguished protest, or awe – these five different attitudes expressing our response to different sorts of namelessness.

First, **it** may be the *unmentionable*. In such idioms as **Rolling in it** and **Up to the neck in it** the familiar Freudian associations of money, faeces, dirt and mud are invoked. They are also hinted at in **Rubbing his nose in it**, **Rubbing it in**, and **You can't take it with you**. *Filthy lucre*. **Don't mention it!**

Secondly, **it** may have a strong sexual charge. It may be the *unspeakable* – which is spoken of much and in great detail in slang. In the sixteenth century **it** was used in slang to mean sexual intercourse. The nineteenth-century use of **it** to mean **just the thing** (**the absolute It, that's exactly it**) was early in the twentieth century transferred to signify exceptional sexual attractiveness or charisma in a woman such as Elinor Glyn or Clara Bow, the 'It-girl'. Kipling has 'Tisn't beauty, so to speak, nor good talk necessarily. It's just it.' (*Traffics and Discoveries, Mrs Bathhurst*). A good contemporary equivalent is: **If you've got it, flaunt it**. Alternatively, **Use it or lose it**. Outstandingly instructive, however, are film titles. Halliwell's standard reference book shows that where **it** is the first word of a film-title, **it** very often turns out to be a space monster. But when **it** occurs *within* the title, it is very often used in order to convey a sexual innuendo – especially a perverse innuendo, which makes this sort of **it** the *unspeakable*. The Internet Movie Database, searching the years 1890–2000, finds 327 titles incorporating *it*. Some uses are weighty: **As It Happened** (1915), **Let It Be** (1970), **Seeing It Through** (1920), *Language Says It All* (1987) – isn't that one *sound*? – and so on. Others from an early date are innocently suggestive, like **At It Again** (1912), **Do It Now** (1924), *Some Like It Hot* (1959), and **As Good As It Gets** (1997). But a startlingly-large number are grossly and violently pornographic, perhaps because the film titles are drawing upon slang expressions. There is an element of rage here.

Thirdly, **it** may be the *unnameable* in the sense of the frightening and monstrous, as in the film *From Hell It Came* (1957). Luther Link, in a recent study of Satan, comments on the paradox that despite the fact that he was an *incubus*, one believed to have intercourse with sleeping women or with witches, Satan never has genitals in Christian art.[8] But his genderlessness makes Satan not less but *more* horrid and fearsome. There is a view – taken up strongly by Freud – that in Western culture, at least, the 'pudenda' have traditionally been seen as shameful and ugly. Georges Bataille, in that tradition, regards the erotic as an **it** for which we feel a mixture of revulsion and awed fascination.[9] But the Freud-Bataille view needs to be revised, because in fact we regard the external indications of gender as friendly, reassuring and humanlike. Fearsome supernatural beings, spirits and monsters, always lack them. In many parts of Europe small images of the male genitalia were used as lucky charms to ward off evil until the Middle Ages, and even later.

Fourthly, **it** may be the *Inevitable* – inscrutable, inflexible Fate, Destiny, Necessity, Kismet. **It** is in theism called the Will, or the decree of God. It is iron or unyielding. It cannot be changed; it has to be accepted. (*Kismet*, from Turkish, comes from the Arabic for one's lot or portion or allocated fate. In the Hebrew Bible the same vocabulary is used. The AV also uses 'lines',[10] from which we get the old-fashioned commiseration, *Hard lines, old chap!*)

Here the point of **it** is not only that we know nothing of the reasons, if any, why people's lots differ so widely, but also that what is neuter cannot be influenced. It is that which cannot be swayed or persuaded to change. We protest against it all the more bitterly for knowing that it is impervious and our protest is vain.

And fifthly, it is sometimes the *Ineffable*, that which is a numinous sacred mystery. In popular religion there is nowadays much emphasis on the personality of God, but in the older and greater tradition impersonal language was very prominent. Not only was God's 'Will' an eternal and immutable decree, but the divine mystery was also spoken of impersonally, as a darkness, an ocean, a desert, a cloud, an abyss, and so on. A great deal of twentieth-century it-talk can therefore be seen as a secularization of the impersonal aspect of the divine.

In summary, then, it may be

(i) Something *unmentionable*, such as dirt or faeces or even money, that we regard as an improper subject of conversation;

(ii) Something *unspeakable*, because it is (perhaps grossly and violently) sexual and hypnotically fascinating to us;

(iii) Something *unnameable* because it is inhuman, un-gendered and monstrous or supernatural, and arouses our fear and horror;

(iv) Something *inevitable* that is unyielding, inscrutable and impervious to our protests and complaints;

or (v) Something *ineffable* that can only be represented by images of a vast impersonal emptiness that fills us with awe.

This analysis may surprise some who do not expect the sacred to be so very close to the unclean, the obscene and the erotic. But in fact religious thought has always been full of sudden and magical reversals and transformations. Even within the Jewish-Christian tradition Satan may transform himself into an angel of light, the highest and holiest may suddenly fall, and the holiest books in the Hebrew Bible are described as 'the books that defile the hands'. Indeed, the reason why religious people get so cross about sex is precisely that religious and sexual feeling are so close to each other.

6

That's it!

It, as we shall see, is different from **life.** In the case of **life** we found that during the past generation or two a wide range of new idioms about **life** have entered the language and have become common currency. Collecting, classifying and interpreting them, we found that life-talk has been modelled on god-talk; that is, the range of things we now say about life corresponds in some detail to the range of things that we used to say about God: we should **commit ourselves to life, trust life, love life, regard life as holy** and as imposing a task upon us, and so on. So **life** appears to be the new religious object, and the relation to **life** is a modern secularization or 'immanentization' of the old relation to God.

Life has a meaning – or at least, a specifiable range of meanings. Life is what biologists study, what actuaries calculate, what biographies are about, and more generally, the way things go in the human life-world, as portrayed in novels and sitcoms. The most general of all the uses of **life** is its use as a near synonym for **It-all,** or **Everything. Life** is **it-all,** as seen from the point or view of a living human creature such as you or me, who is in it and part of **it-all,** and whose viewpoint is the only comprehensive viewpoint there is. One might consider defining **life** as the *Lebensweltgeist*, the spirit that animates the whole **life-world.**

In this last use **life, It-all** and **Everything** are rather pantheistic and Spinozistic. When we ask **How are things? How's life with you? How is it going with you?** we seem to be asking a person how she feels about her place in the whole scheme of things of which she is part. Is she comfortable with the way things are going for her? Is she **with it** or has she **lost it**? **How is it with her?** How is everything in general treating her, and does she feel that **her life is going somewhere** (as opposed to '**My life is going nowhere**')?

Life then has a meaning, or at least, a fairly clear range of meanings, and in some of its peripheral uses **life** overlaps with **it**. **How's life?** can be interchangeable with **How's it going?** But **it** does not have a meaning, merely a very large and almost-sinister range of idiomatic uses, which turn out to be difficult to classify in any way that helps to explain why the word is so disturbing. Even the simplest idioms may suddenly strike one as very odd, or turn out to have unexpectedly strong theological or religious overtones.

For example: **It is hot.** Here 'it' figures as 'the subject of an impersonal statement of a condition of things, without reference to any agent'. At first glance this sounds like a coolly objective scientific observation-report. The speaker leaves out any reference to himself, and says in a general and impersonal way that 'hot' is how it just is today, as any trained observer will confirm. Yes, indeed; I wasn't just saying or complaining that I happen to *feel* hot, but that *it* objectively *is* hot. But then, what *is* this **it** that is objectively hot? **All this,** or circumstances in general, or the weather? – And now one is reminded of the old observation that in parts of Africa, where we might say 'it', they say 'God'. Geoffrey Parrinder makes the point in a way that reminds us of the prominence of prayers about the weather in the English Prayer Books:

The Supreme Being is in heaven and so he is particularly concerned with rain, upon which men depend entirely for their life. He is rarely associated with the sun, for in the tropics the sun is always present, and there is no need of chants and sacrifices to bring the sun back again, as in ancient Europe and Japan. God rends the sky with lightning and moves the forest so that the trees murmur. Instead of saying 'it', as we do when we say 'it is hot', Africans often say 'God is fiercely hot', 'God is falling as rain', 'God makes the drumming of thunder'. To say 'God is burying eggs' means that as a crocodile hides eggs in the sand and comes back later without mistake, so the thunder will return in time. When rain begins the pleasant freshness is described by saying that 'God has softened the day'. The rainbow is often called 'the bow of God', who is like a hunter.

God is high and over all things, he 'covers' us like the sky.[11]

This in turn reminds us that something similar can be said in English, when we totalize all our circumstances and view them as either being wonderfully benign ('God's in his heaven / All's right with the world'), or as seeming to conspire against us (*Someone up there is telling me something*, or **God's got it in for me**). Nowadays this sort of language is used only facetiously; but the fact that it can be used at all indicates that the use of **it** in 'It is hot' still has detectable theological overtones. It is as if we are saying that it is hot *for me*. When we say that 'It is hot' we invoke the idea of a viewpoint that is general and objective, a God's-eye-view, the viewpoint of One who is neither a man nor a woman, but something universal. And perhaps I am saying that the hotness I feel is being *sent* to me by **it**. We still tend to take weather-conditions as signs of favour or disfavour towards us. The weather is 'clement' to *us*, the sun smiles upon *us*. Because the weather's moods directly influence our own moods, we may feel that **it** is *telling us* something.

For a second example of the way even the simplest it-idioms may have religious overtones I take **This is it** and **That's it**. **This is it** is used to say that some event long awaited and hoped-for is now at last taking place. Exactly what we have been needing and desiring is now accessible: **Don't miss it**. Seize the moment – and of course we now realize that **This is it** is eschatological: it says that the time is fulfilled, Now is the hour.

As for **That's it**, it is used to say *No more, I've had enough*, **It's all over, That's the end of it**. **That's it** is used, as they say, *to close a chapter*, and therefore implies something like a dispensationalist view of time. In fact, **that is it** is so serious that it seems almost to announce the end of the world, as the novelist Anthony Burgess noted when borrowing the title of an apocalypse-novel from the traditional BBC World Service announcement that *That is the end of the World News.*[12] In Britain, we would be upset if the newsreader ended the bulletin with the abrupt and terrifying **That's it,** so he and she are oblig-ed to smile a little wryly and say **Well, that's about it,** or, **That's all from me for now,** or, even more bathetically, **Well: that about wraps it up for now.** And the very need to resort to such grimacing and apologetic circumlocutions bears eloquent testi-mony to the hinted-at religious violence and finality of even such little phrases as **This is it** and **That's it.**

Now a third example, taken from the group of phrases **Go for it, Get at it, Make it, Get it?, Got it** and **Got what it takes.** We began on page 7 with the use of **it** to signify something whose identity is being withheld: something nameless and fear-some, alien and perhaps supernatural. But language has a way of flipping over to the opposite extreme, and there are many uses of **it** to signify something that is not described because it doesn't *need* to be described. It is so specific, so welcome, so unmistakably what we are looking for, and so immediately recognized by everyone that it needs no description. It is, as the Victorians used to say, **The absolute It.** These uses of **it** are associated not with anything dark and dreadful but with public success and good fortune or personal *charisma.* **Get to it!, Go for it, Get at it, You are going to make it** (= get there, succeed or survive), **Get it?** (= do you understand?), **Got it!** (= by a sudden inspiration I have found the answer; I have obtained what I was seeking). **She's got it,** said of a woman between about the 20s and the 70s of the past century (and still some-times heard) ascribed to her compelling and charismatic sexual attractiveness; and **He's got what it takes** means that he has exactly the qualities required; he is just the man for the job, the right stuff.

In this group of idioms, **it** is, as we've said, not something dark and potentially dreadful, but something shining, highly public and instantly recognizable. But here **it** is *still* religious, and our vocabulary shows it. It is the quality of being a *star*, an *icon*, a *high flier*, someone who is *charismatic* in the ancient sense of being endued with divine grace and favour, and therefore destined for great things.

But now a fourth and last example, which again shows a reversal of meanings and associations. We were just now associating it with **the very thing**, just what we wanted, and therefore with shining success and star-quality. But another group of very simple idioms associates it with a leaden sense of failure, fatigue and loss of nerve: **It's no good, It's no use, It won't do, I can't go on with it, What's the point of it all?, It's beyond me, It's hopeless, It's too late, I've had it, It's all over.**

Something like this may be said by a person who has lost the thread of his life. He's lost his project; he is no longer **with it.** He cannot **see any point in it.** At the next stage he may try to shake off his low spirits by **making light of it. It doesn't matter. It can't be helped. It just wasn't to be. You do your best, and where does it get you? It's all a bit too much for me. It's all going horribly wrong. It's getting me down. Things are getting on top of me.**

At the next stage he makes a violent effort to throw off the incubus. **Forget it. God damn it all. Blast it. Curse it. F--- it. Blow it.**

Then he begins to simmer down and approach a mood of resignation. **Life's a pig, isn't it? I ask you, is it worth it? Well, can you see any purpose behind it all? It only shows. I'll just have to put up with it. There's not a lot I can do about it. It could be worse. Perhaps it's all been for the best. Maybe it's been a blessing in disguise.** And finally, in a mood of acceptance, **So be it, Let it be, It's going to be all right. Amen to that.**

And so we begin to see how the it-idioms differ from the life-idioms. When we studied life-talk we found that the word *life* does have a (fairly clear) meaning, or range of meanings, and that life-talk is modelled in some detail on God-talk. Life-talk proved to be *theologically* classifiable. It-talk is turning out to be rather different. *It* has no meaning. **It** is something more like a nameless, ungendered and perhaps impersonal background to our life upon which we vent our feelings. It is something like our invisible antagonist, against which or whom we must play the game of life. Above all, It attracts expression and draws out our feelings. The it-idioms can only be classified in terms of the great range of moods and emotions that they express and evoke; and where have we met that range of emotions and moods before? – in the Psalter. Perhaps there is a connection between It and ancient ideas about God? Is not God the ultimate **thing-in-itself**?

7

A game of chess, played against an invisible opponent

Earlier (p.10 above), I suggested the hypothesis that **it** is a sort of Joker-word which because it has no specific meaning of its own can in its numberless idiomatic uses be used to mean almost anything and can evoke almost any emotion. The Joker-word opens a crack in the world and makes us shiver.

Just now, though, I have suggested a slightly different hypothesis. Language's first use is for conversation with others, and it is not surprising that when we are talking about **what we are up against**, we should wish to semi-personify **it**. In *The New Religion of Life* we noted Virginia Woolf saying how important it is to establish some sort of communication with an invisible universal Other:

> The interest in life does not lie in what people do, nor even in their relations to each other, but largely in the power to communicate with a third party, antagonistic, enigmatic, yet perhaps persuadable, which one may call life itself.[13]

In the Life-book I saw this text as being about **Life**. Now, I prefer to fasten upon the word **itself**. When we are really **up against it**, we may well wish to articulate our feelings about **it**, and semi-personification helps. The third person singular is he, she or **it**, and **itself** – a very-long-established term, by the way – follows *himself* and *herself*, suggesting that **it** too may perhaps have some kind of selfhood.

The image of our human life as being a battle of wits, a game of chess played against an invisible opponent, seems to come from Thomas Henry Huxley and to coincide with the beginnings of modern agnosticism. The great growth in the number of it-idioms since about 1870 seems to suggest that people in general have found at least some features of god-talk to be indispensable. The process of human life needs to be contextualized; that is, we need some way of representing the backdrop of life, and the way things may seem sometimes to be going against us, and at other times to be running in our favour. The it-idioms do the job very well, and the continuing influence of theism shows up in the way an atheist will say humorously *God does exist after all!* when he hears that some villain or political opponent has got his much-needed and overdue comeuppance. **It**, one may say, includes God and is prior to God, so that **it** will, just sometimes, deliver the just deserts and the poetic revenge that one rejoices to see. Indeed, the it-idioms are so wideranging and varied that they incorporate not only the old theistic vision but also the old tragic-fate vision of things, and the old luck-and-fortune vision as well. **It** is perhaps becoming the modern person's replacement for God, Fate, Luck and **the way of it,** all bundled into one. **So it goes. That's how it is.**

Can we write the history of **it** in more detail? A friend has urged me to find out when the use of *it* to make general statements about the weather began: **It is hot, It's foul** and so on. He may have thought that **It is hot** began around 1660 or so, at the time of the founding of the Royal Society, when the scientific way of reporting events was coming in and gentlemen began keeping weather records. But, for once, Homer nodded, for that particular use of **it** goes back to Saxon times – and so does **itself,** at least in some such form as **hit selfe.** So the historical hypothesis will have to be as follows: Western culture is a mongrel, and there never was a period when theism entirely dominated ordinary language. In ordinary language people have always expressed their sense of the way of things in an eclectic mixture of God-talk, Fate-talk, Luck-talk and It-talk. They still do: remember the highly-successful commercials for the National Lottery, with the giant Hand and the deep Voice saying **It could be you?** But since about the time of T. H. Huxley there has been a considerable expansion of It-idioms, to such an extent that we seem by now to admit that **It** is logically primary, and that God-talk perhaps evolved by way of persuading people to **think well of it** and **make the best of it**. God is or was, in the Western Christian world, the human face of **It**, perhaps, in which case to believe in God is to believe that **it** is One, consistent and friendly to us.

Since William James first associated the defence of religious faith with the defence of optimism, it has become something of a psychological commonplace that it is healthy and rational, because it is profitable, to take a slightly over-optimistic view of things – of one's own abilities, attractiveness and life-expectancy for example, and similarly of the qualities of one's friends, or students, or children. We will tend to justify our own optimism by trying to live up to our own expectations for ourselves, and other people similarly will tend to try to live up to our expectations of them. So it comes about that the person who says that *You can't trust other people* tends to find himself living in a world in which other people indeed cannot be trusted, whereas the person who prefers to like and trust others tends to end up in a world that justifies her faith. The optimist ends up better off, and is therefore right.

Applying the same principles at the cosmological level, we may say that **it** is primary, and is enigmatic. Pessimists say about **it** that **It never rains but it pours**, whereas optimists say that **It's an ill wind that blows nobody any good. Makes you sick, doesn't it?**, says the pessimist: **Maybe it'll all come out right in the end,** says the optimist. Anyway, **It could be worse.** The pessimist retorts ruefully with Margaret Thatcher's words on the day she was forced out of office: **It's a funny old world.** It is always enigmatic and ambiguous. Against this familiar background, one might see a good deal of popular belief since William James as siding with his view that faith in God expresses a decision consistently to try to *Look on the bright side of life* and **Make the best of it**. Then, having made that decision, we must **See it through**, perseveringly.

We may or may not find James's style of apologetics – theistic

faith equals persistent **it**-optimism – congenial, but there is certainly **a lot of it about** nowadays, and its rationality is often
defended by Jamesian arguments. True beliefs are the beliefs
that are good for you: **it** – optimism is good for you; therefore
belief in God, as **it**-optimism, is true. So runs the main argument. And my present point is that even if you are a perfectly
sincere Jamesian theist, you are still tacitly conceding the logical
and philosophical priority of **It** over God. Jamesian apologetics
cannot even be stated without conceding that point.[14]

I take it, then, that the predominance of it-idioms in modern
popular speech demonstrates that deep-down we now generally
accept the primacy of **It**. Some of us (mainly the poor) are still
much drawn to talk about Luck and Fortune, and others of us
(mainly the *bien-pensants*) profess belief in God; and people in
both groups may sincerely claim that their personal experience
of life has given them at least a Jamesian justification for their
faith. It's a source of happiness: it gives them something to trust
and to hope for. Very well: **It figures. Have it your own way.**
But all along language now whispers to us the far superior
weight and numbers of the it-idioms. It now comes first. **That's
about the size of it. That's the gist of it.**

8

Accepting it, or Fighting it?

How far do our it-idioms show us taking up religious attitudes towards it? It is clear at once, even from the few idioms so far quoted, that we are instructed by our language to **face up to it, come to terms with it, make our peace with it, accept it** and become **resigned**, or **reconciled to it** so that we can eventually say Amen, **So be it,** without bitterness. But is that enough to make it appropriate to think of **it** as being in some way the religious object? After all, **it** is not personal, or not quite personal: we don't speak of having faith in **it**, and we don't speak either of **it** as loving us, or of ourselves as in any serious sense loving **it**. There is indeed a light sense of '**loving it**', by which we mean taking great and unexpected pleasure in some specific and finite thing; but **it** in the weighty sense is something that one bows to, or something that after a religious struggle one becomes at last ready to accept and say Amen to. **It leaves us with no options. There are no two ways about it. We just have to put up with it. We can't argue with it. We must accept it.**

In the idioms just quoted, **it** seems to mean the human condition in general, its finitude and its context or backdrop. **It** also includes events that are cosmic for the individual affected by them, because they **change everything** and we must simply reconcile ourselves to them. By this I mean such events as learning that I or somebody very close to me has a terminal illness, and other events that have a similar tragic finality about them.

In theism we have always seen the struggle to come to terms with such events as a religious struggle, culminating in *Islam*, submission, or in the *Amen* of Jesus in Gethsemane. One strives with God, and in the end says, 'Thy Will be done'. In theism, **it**

is described as 'the Will of God': **accept it as the Will of God**, as
the phrase goes. But when the old realistic belief in God goes,
and we are left **to cope with it**, do we still need to struggle to
reconcile ourselves to **it**, and is the struggle still a *religious*
struggle?

Hearing that a lady named Margaret Fuller had stated: 'I
accept the Universe', Thomas Carlyle is alleged to have
exclaimed, 'Gad! She'd better!' – meaning presumably that since
we are stuck with our lot and have no choice in the matter, it is
as otiose to say 'I accept the Universe' as it would be to say 'I
reject the Universe', and religion **hardly comes into it**.

I disagree with Carlyle. First, because Islam is to such a large
extent a religion of devout submission to **It**, and nobody doubts
that Islam is a great and very potent religion. In Islam, God is
not a Father, and there is very little of the answers to prayer, the
healing miracles and the 'particular providences' that play so
large a part in popular Catholic Christian piety. If, as I suggested earlier, in Christianity 'God is the human face of It', it
should be added that in Islam God does not have any such
human face. God comes near to being equated with **It**: yet Islam
is religion. And secondly, there is a real dispute between those
who see our relation to **It** in terms of, say, the struggle of
Tolstoy's *Ivan Ilyich* to reach a religious acceptance of his own
death, and those on the other hand who say on the contrary that
we should **fight it to the end**, and quote Dylan Thomas's *Do not
go gentle into that good night*. There is, I repeat, a real dispute
between those who want **to fight it all the way** and those who
seek **to accept it**. This is a very big dispute, which affects our
whole view of life from beginning to end. Who is the better and
happier human being, the fighter or the one who **goes along
with it**: and which attitude to life do the idioms endorse?

The answer to this is that perhaps the balance between the
two responses is changing. Historically our great religions were
unanimous in recommending submission to **it**, and militant,
defiant 'it-atheism' seems to have become widely popular only
since about the time of the publication of Dylan Thomas's
poem, *Do not go gentle into that good night*. The obvious

phrases are related to phrases that encouraged soldiers to fight, and 'to fight for dear life'.

Go to it!
Go for it! Get at it!
Don't let it get you down
Tackle it head-on
Fight it all the way
Keep it up!
Face up to it

People are very widely praised for putting up a brave fight, particularly against serious illness and physical handicap; and people who die of cancer are more often than not praised for having **fought it to the end**. Do you recall a popular music hall song: *Keep right on to the end of the road*? It was sung by Sir Harry Lauder in the 1940s.

The **fight-it** idioms are, it appears, of very recent origin. Perhaps they are associated with the National Health Service and the power of modern medicine, which have given the **fight-it** policy a better chance of success than it used to have. In earlier times it was the unbeliever destined for hell who had to be dragged kicking and screaming over the threshold of death and then down to Hades, like Don Juan – all of which meant that fighting death was viewed by others as a symptom of probable damnation. The believer was praised for dying peacefully: peace of mind in death was thought to be evidence that you were one of the Elect, destined for eternal salvation. And the influence of that long tradition still survives in our idioms: they tell us that we will be happiest if we accept the inescapable limits of the human condition as if they are God's will for us. A peaceful death is *a good death*. I have already quoted a number of the phrases that urge us to make our peace with **it**. **It** is inescapable: we cannot hope to get the better of **it**.

It catches up with us
Don't run away from it
Come to terms with it
Accept it
Resign yourself to it
Become reconciled to it
Amen / So be it / Let it be
We can't argue with it
We just have to put up with it
There are no two ways about it
You can't have it both ways
It leaves us no options
There's not a lot you can do about it
(He should have known) He had it coming to him
It's got my name on it
It's down to me
That's how it goes (Fr., *ça va*)
It can't be helped
Now you've done it
He's had it
It won't do
It has to be
See it through
He won't get away with it
It's a shame
It shouldn't happen to a dog
It's beyond me
Get it over and done with

Lest this list be thought oppressive and near fatalistic, I should report at once the joy with which I heard the first clear example I have found of *it non-realism*: It depends on how you look at it (compare It's all in the mind, It all depends, Oh no, it isn't!). But that is enough: stop it!

9

Phrases about dealing with It

In the life-book, sayings about *life* that were not relevant to the book's main line of argument were simply left out of consideration, without any comment or explanation. Here **it seems better** to adopt the other policy and to give at least a brief account of all the main kinds of it-idiom.

Many it-idioms, then, are not cosmically general. They are turns of speech. **It** signifies the matter that is of current concern, the business in hand or the project that is under way. The idioms fall into four main groups: some are about *appraising* it, some urge one to **get on with it** and **get it done**, some voice the feeling that **it's all too much** and **I can't go on with it**, and the last group, concerned with consolation, say in one way and another that **it doesn't matter**, and you'll **get over it** in time.

We note that discouragement or anxiety about some finite **it** may 'go cosmic'. Then we start complaining not just about **it**, but about **it all**, that is, **everything**. And then the voice of consolation usually tries to scale down our anxiety and **get it into perspective**.

So we now review the main stages of the standard psychodrama of the relation between the self and **It**. The details require close study.

(i)   Appraising **it**

  The gist of it
  The long and short of it
  That's about the size of it
  By the sound of it

By the looks of it
He's got it bad for her
It's a hard life
If it comes to it
It rather depends / It all depends
It can't happen here
It is a question of
It looks like it
It happens
It isn't what it was
Whatever it is
I can't believe it
It's a boy! / It's a girl!
Make it clear / Make it plain
It seems to be so
It is the case that . . .
Does it all add up?
Maybe it'll all turn out right in the end
It's as simple as that
It wasn't as straightforward as that
It's later than you think
It's a small world
It's really quite something
On the face of it
He'll never get away with it
What is it? (= what's the trouble?)
It'll never do

(ii)   Getting on with it

Go for it!
You'll soon pick it up
Get on with it!
Get it right!
Get down to it
Getting around to it
Get with it!

Just do it!
Get it done!
Use it or lose it!
It's dogged as does it
Push it to the limit
Is he up to it?
Give it up!
See it through
Put it down on paper
Put it across (i.e., communicate it)
Play it by ear
Take it easy
Hard at it
Making it
Make it up[15] / Cheat it
Run for it
Leave it to me
Go it alone
Go it blind (i.e., double the ante without looking at the cards)
Take it from here
See to it
It takes two to tango

(beginning to **turn against it**)

It's later than you think
It's more than my job's worth
I can take it or leave it / I can do without it
It doesn't do to do that
It ill becomes him to do that
It won't do

(iii)   **It's all becoming too much**

It's all I can do to do (something)
It's as much as I can do to do (something)
It's beyond me
It's too dangerous now

It's too late now
I can't keep it up
I can't help it
I'm up against it
I can't take any more of it
I can't make any sense of it
It's all a bit too much for me
It's getting me down
It's getting on top of me
It is very hard to deal/cope with . . .
It beats me!

(and the sense of defeat begins to turn cosmic, as – for example
– it becomes it all)

It's all a bit too much
It's all going horribly wrong
What's the point of it all?
I can't take it all in
What does it all mean?
Can you see any point behind it all?
What's it all about?
Where will it all end?
It just doesn't add up
I've had it
I don't care about it
I can take it or leave it

(iv)   Consolation: the comforter may seek to 'de-cosmicize' it
so as to cut it down to size.

We need to Get away from it all.

It doesn't matter
It's not the end of the world
It's only money
It's only a game
Get it into perspective

You must just put up with it
Grin and bear it
You'll get over it
There's not all that much to it
It's going to be all right
It doesn't count
Maybe it just wasn't to be
It's just as well
It's an ill wind that blows nobody any good
It is better to have loved and lost than never to have loved at all
It's over and done with
It's a funny old world!
It's all in a day's work

(wonder or no wonder, in calmer retrospect)

It's no wonder that
Makes you wonder, though, doesn't it?
Is it any wonder?
It/that remains to be seen

This selection of it-idioms treats it as signifying generally that which I'm up against, that with which I have to deal. It is the self's finite (and usually impersonal) Other – a state of affairs, a prospect, a memory, a vocation, a task, a business, any matter of current concern. At all times, our well-being depends upon our maintaining confidence that we can measure it up rightly, cope with it, see it through and come to the end of it. When confidence falters, instead of my being on top of it, it looms larger and larger, and threatens to get on top of me. When confidence fails altogether, It becomes It-all, fills the world and defeats me, or gets me down. I feel I want to give it up, or pack it in. I'd give anything to get it over and done with.

One strand of popular wisdom strives to rebuild shattered confidence: It's not as bad as all that. But another and more important strand of popular wisdom urges us to be tough-minded and to acknowledged that Life's a pig, innit?, that It can't be helped, that we should **Put it down to experience,** and acknowledge that final defeat and loss are our fate. **There's not a lot you can do about it.** You have to just **grin and bear it.**

Generally speaking, ruling-class ideologies, both political and religious, preach optimism downwards. The whole scheme of things, **It All,** is ultimately rational and benevolent, so that if you faithfully do your duty to the end, **it** will reward you. But the popular wisdom takes a more pessimistic view, valuing resignation and endurance: **Don't let it get you down.** A 'good sense of humour' and a little gambling, 'trusting to luck', make **it all** easier to bear. **Stick it out.**

10

The mystery of It

Soon after the painter René Magritte died in 1967, his widow Georgette said this about him:

> He thought there was a mystery in the world. When he was talking with Paul Collinet I often heard him say: 'There is a mystery in the universe, but what is it?'[16]

That's right: there is a mystery, but we don't know what it is – chiefly because we locate it in entirely the wrong place. We don't know **where it's at**. We tend to think that ordinariness is clear and unproblematic. Around the ordinary life-world are the various territories that are described by the technical vocabularies of the sciences, and then, beyond the humanly-mapped world and the limits of scientific knowledge, mysteries begin. So in earlier times the accurately-mapped and 'known' world of men was surrounded by a vague *terra incognita* swarming with monsters.

The true position is almost the exact reverse of this. First – and for reasons that I have given elsewhere and will not repeat here – there is no mysterious realm lying 'beyond' the human world, just as there is no place North of the North Pole, because the humanly-known and mapped world, though finite, is unbounded and outsideless. Secondly, the technical language of science is as simple, clear and unambiguous as language can be made to be. And thirdly, the deepest mystery is hidden at the very centre of ordinariness, where language becomes quite bewilderingly opaque, knotted and forceful, and even the simplest-seeming expressions defeat us.

I am the sort of person who can be kept awake all night by

the baffling gentle beauty of a phrase like *coming to be*. Two years ago, on the night in question, it was the word *coming* that whispered itself to me over and over. Where was this coming *coming from*, as **it** comes *into being*? Finally, in the Being-books, the *coming* and the *be* were conflated in Be-ing as pure transience (= going by, or 'passing'). Now, I have had another wakeful night over two it-idioms of mind-boggling beauty: **The way of it**, or **That's the way it is** and, even lovelier, **It came to pass** . . .

Was there ever a time when people truly experienced the mysterious as something invisible and timeless? I doubt it: at any rate, I say now that the **mystery of It-all** is the mystery of Being, which is the mystery of **Its** way of coming and passing. **It happens**, that's **how it is** (*Comment c'est*, a Beckett title). As for 'passing', everyone seems to love and to need the idea: it is German *passieren* and French *passer*; it is Asia's universal 'impermanence' (*anicca/anitya*).

No doubt the poets have always experienced language as dense, knotted, alive, opaque and world-filling; but only very recently has that same sense of language begun to spread more widely, and to obsess philosophers. Wittgenstein writes very well, but I no longer find in him quite what I currently feel. The new sense of language is post-Lacan, and perhaps much more recent even than that.

It is not easy to share this, but try taking word by word the following little string of it-idioms. They poleaxe me:

It is. It isn't. Isn't it? It can't be. But it's so. So it is.

When we refer to *what is so*, we seem to invoke a common public it-world, a world in which **it is the case**, a neuter/neutral world of public facts that can be appealed to to settle arguments. Imagine then my shock at again hearing delighted children at the pantomime, shouting the old exchange over and over again:

Oh yes, it is! Oh no, it isn't!

Having heard that, again I find that **I don't know what it is.** I confess that **It is a complete mystery to me.** Perhaps the reason is that although we continually posit **It** as an objective Other, and declare that we are **up against it,** it remains oddly elusive. **Would you believe it? The cheek of it!** The problem is that **when you come down to it,** or **get down to it, it** is not only knotty and difficult, but also obscure and evasive. It's transient. **I don't hold with it:** it slips away. **It all frightens me,** by this weird combination of dark knottiness and slipperiness. **Would you believe it?** I don't. I envy those people who feel able to say **I never give it a thought.** I keep asking **What's it like?** and I get no answer. Language somehow refuses to tell me. **That's the worst of it.** There isn't an objective public **It** that can be invoked to settle disagreements, because, as everyone knows, **It all depends** – ordinary language's version of thoroughgoing relativism. *It all depends:* is that not *simply* beautiful?

Scientific realism claims that scientific knowledge is as near as we'll ever get to absolute knowledge. Natural science describes an independently-real surrounding it-world that we can appeal to to settle arguments, and with which we must and can be content. And it is assumed that ordinary people are 'natural' realists, who will be very happy to accept these claims.

I do not agree. As we will see at several points, ordinary language is curiously uninterested in precisely-described objective facts. It has an acute sense of relativity, contingency, mystery. And its chief concern is always with individual and corporate *morale*. It seeks to build and maintain the emotional strength to love life and live well. In philosophy, it is closest to existentialism. And finally, ordinary language does not look to **it** for comfort and consolation. Not at all.

11

The purely-descriptive **it**?

In section 9 above, 'Phrases about dealing with It', the human being appeared as *homo faber*, man the worker, actively engaged with the world. **Whatever it was**, he wrestled with **it** like Jacob wrestling with the angel. He must either **stay on top of it** or **it would get him down** and then it would **get on top of him**. **It** was like the hard intractable land from which he must *wrest* a living: **It** was like the obdurate stiffnecked working animal that he must tame and bend to his will, because **if he didn't master it, it would master him**. And one might also say that **It** was like the equally-difficult gods, spirits and other supernatural powers that Bronze-Age man also had to struggle with and come to terms with. For this predictable unpredictability of things, this knack of being bloody awkward every time, people still use phrases like **Would you believe it?** (or, **Would you Adam-'n-Eve it?**) and **Makes you sick, doesn't it?**, or **Ain't it marvellous?**

Thus ordinary language still preserves in some detail the very-archaic – one might say, early Neolithic – view of the world as a scrimmage of powers and forces, and of human life as a struggle for well-being and survival against a many-headed **It**. That is **how it is** for most ordinary folk still, even in what are too-flatteringly called the 'advanced' countries. One struggles to survive, one **battles against it**, one **grins and bears it**, and one keeps up one's spirits by buying a Lottery ticket. Life is hard labour, but after **it** there is rest.

Thus the not-self out-there, **It**, has for at least six thousand years been perceived as an obdurate, cussed, non-human force or power or aggregate of forces and powers. If there ever was an Age of Gold, it is long past now. The Universe is not a free lunch: we are **up against it** and must struggle to survive. **It's tough, It's a hard life,** *Isn't life a terrible thing, thank God?* Some idioms voice a sharp protest: **I can't bear it, It's a disgrace, I can't stand it, It's not fair.** But other idioms say that **it is idle to complain;** for example, **I thought it pointless to protest;** *Everything is what it is, and not another thing;*[17] and anyway, **That's the way it goes. So it is.** *So it goes.*[18]

And so things were for the ordinary person from the early Neolithic until the arrival in the mid-twentieth century of the fully-technological society, and so, for many or most people, **it remains.** In which case, **how comes it** that is an impersonal purely-descriptive **It** has also been established in the language since quite early Iron Age times? In the English language, the *OED* (1991, s.v.) traces the impersonal **it** back into Old English/Anglo-Saxon, citing, for example, **It is hot, it is cold** from Alfred and **It rains** and **It snows** from Bede. Before then, the it-idioms come at least from Latin predecessors and especi-ally from the Gospels, where, in the sayings of Jesus especially, the action of God is heavily-veiled behind it-idioms: of Judas, for example, Jesus says: 'Woe to that man by whom the Son of Man is betrayed! **It were better for him that he had never been born**' (Matthew 26.24, AV). Jesus will not eat with his disciples again until '**it is fulfilled** in the kingdom of God' (Luke 22.15). On the cross, he cries: '**It is finished**' (John 19.30). Walking to Emmaus, the Risen Jesus says to the disciples: '**Was it not necessary that** the Christ should suffer these things and enter into his glory?' (Luke 24.26). In other languages such as Greek and Hebrew we do not of course find exact counterparts of English it-idioms; but just the same job is very often done by a passive construction or by the use of periphrasis. Thus, instead of *God will do A*, we read that *A will be done* or that *It will come about that A*. The motive for this veiled way of speaking may be reverence, or fear, or a sense of what is decent and fitting; and the matter thus veiled might be sacred, or it might be concerned with sex or with death or some other highly-charged concern. The extent to which Jesus' sayings conceal divine action behind it-idioms and passive constructions has never been much remarked upon by theologians because for most of the past seventeen centuries the Bible has been read with a very strong dogmatic interest: everything Jesus carefully hides, the Church has struggled to make highly explicit, and then to impose by law as a test of faith. (From the very first, the Church got Jesus *radically* wrong). But through such expressions as **It is written** one is encouraged to trace it-idioms back further, into the Hebrew scriptures, and to ask the question: How did they begin?

The answer seems to be threefold. (i) It-idioms could be used to describe God's finished work, viewed as if from God's point of view: *God saw everything that he had made, and, behold, it was very good* (Genesis 1.21). (ii) Thereafter, it-idioms gradually develop along with other narrative techniques. They set the scene for a story, as in '*And it came to pass at that time . . .*' (Genesis 21.22, c.f. 22.1, 27.1, etc.). Exact dates come to be added: '*Now it came to pass in the month Chislev, in the twentieth year, as I was in Shushan the palace . . .*' (Nehemiah 1.1). (iii) When historical testimony gets to be as detailed as that, it reminds one of the evidence given under oath by a witness in court. As we have remarked, **It** is often disputable: **I don't believe it!** declares one, and **I don't doubt it** retorts another. In court, the use of an oath backed by religious sanctions, and of a carefully weighed third-person style – it was thus and so – shows the court's need to do all it can to determine a public truth and arrive at a public verdict. The Torah demanded the evidence of at least two witnesses before a defendant could be convicted (Deuteronomy 19.15, etc.), and they had to agree about the relevant facts. A defendant like Susannah, who had dismissed her maid on the occasion in question, could not call upon any human witness to back up her story. She had no other recourse than to call upon God: 'as God is my witness'. As for the two elders, they would have won their case if they had told the same story; but one said that it was under a mastic tree that Susannah and the unnamed young man were fornicating, and the other that it was under a holm oak. So they lost – which shows how much courts need to pursue a third-person sort of public truth, however hard it is **to establish it**. (See the account of the trial in Susannah vv.28–62.)

Thus (as we noticed earlier, on page 0) the descriptive **It** is much more ancient than first thoughts might suggest. Its two main uses are in story-telling and in bearing witness, and in both cases there is a dimly-suggested theological background: **God made it so**. From a God's-eye view, **that's how it looks**, and therefore **that's how it is**.

It may also happen that an individual uses an it-idiom in speaking of himself. The idiom has a throat-clearing and attention-demanding function. Here are five examples:

It strikes me that . . .
It has often occurred to me that . . .
It has come to my notice that . . .
It is idle to deny that . . .
It was necessary to decide to do such-and-such

To use very old-fashioned language, these idioms are almost blasphemous. The individual veils himself as Jesus veils God, merely in order to add weight to his opinions, or to exculpate his actions by suggesting that he was under some kind of constraint. I will waste no more space upon the second really-unpleasant group of it-idioms that we have yet found.[19]

12

The tragedy of it

We have been proposing a sharp distinction between **the way it looks** to the ordinary human being who is actively engaged with life, **hard at it** and more-or-less continually **up against it**, and **the way it looks** from the more disengaged perspective of such figures as the old person recounting memories of **how it was in my day**, the story-teller who begins by saying that **it came to pass**, the journalist **reporting it as it happens**, the judge hearing evidence about **it** in a court case, and more recently the trained scientific observer. Overwhelmingly, ordinary language speaks of **it** in the tones of someone who is actively struggling with **it**. He is concerned about one thing only: what it is like to be struggling as he is, and whether the tide of battle is running with him or against him. But the neutrally descriptive **it** of memory, story-telling, testimony and science has since early times been there too, as a special language-game that is appropriate in certain special contexts.

We have suggested that **Life**, in ordinary language, is now something like the whole ongoing process of things in the human life-world. Life might even be called the *Lebensweltgeist*. **It**, in ordinary language, is what-we-are-up-against. **It** is Virginia Woolf's 'third party': **it** is that enigmatic cussedness of things that *makes life difficult* for us: **it** is life's unknown, uncomprehended but determining backdrop. **It** is whatever's out there, silent and implacable.

Further investigation of the relation between **It** and **Life** must be deferred for the present. Here we raise a prior question: apart from certain special descriptive language games, is ordinary language concerned about descriptive truth *at all*? Might it not be that ordinary language, the ancient core and heart of all language, is entirely expressive and emotive? Do not my 450 or so it-idioms show that the ordinary human being engaged with life is not in the least interested in **what it is**? If you ask him '**What is it?**', you will get in reply an expression of his feelings, and perhaps a demand for encouragement and sympathy. You'll certainly not get a technical scientific description of **it**. Indeed, you don't expect one, for your question '**What is it?**' was not a scientific enquiry: it was the offer of a sympathetic ear.

I am suggesting that not only our it-idioms and our life idioms, but ordinary language in general shows almost no interest in knowledge or in detailed descriptions. Ordinary language seems to be *phatic*, that is, it is used entirely to facilitate social interaction of various kinds. We use it to commune with others, sharing our feelings, voicing our complaints and enlisting the sympathy, cooperation and support of others. Hence the lack of interest in what **it** is. We know **it's hell**; that's all we care.

In the Western cultural and educational tradition that descends from Plato it has always been thought that a concern for *knowledge* is distinctively human, and indeed is of the first importance to us. It has been supposed that if indeed knowledge comes first, then simple descriptive statements like 'The cat sits on the mat' can be taken as typical examples of ordinary language. To us Platonists it is disconcerting to think that knowledge may have been radically overestimated. Functionally, the core of human language is still the same as animal communication. It is used to procure social cooperation and to maintain social harmony, and it is used to express feelings and to demand help and encouragement. But it is not used to formulate general truths, nor to develop a theory of the world. Hence the mysteriousness of **it**: *it-agnosticism* is not a conclusion reached after reflection, but represents merely a profound lack of interest. The concern for knowledge and truth is not original in human beings, but rather represents a secondary and very specialized development. We could have lived without it; and many do.

It is worth asking whether there are any significant exceptions to all this: does ordinary idiom actually include any notable empirical generalizations about **how it is**, generalizations about the world or about human nature that we may regard as having been thoroughly tested in common experience? Does the popular wisdom include anything that could be called knowledge? I search my lists of it-idioms, and find such items as these:

> **It is dogged as does it**
> **It is never too late to mend**
> **It is love that makes the world go round**
> **It is best not to get too involved**
> **It is just like/quite unlike him to have done that**
> **It never rains but it pours**
> **It is all in a day's work**

These items are of no relevance to our present point. They are very general comments, encouragements and recommendations, but so far as they make any empirical claim, it can – as always in these cases – be countered by other sayings and proverbs that say just the opposite. From the Bronze Age to the present day the popular wisdom has always been rather unsystematic. To have a good stock of proverbs, and to have the knack of producing the right one on the right occasion, is to have a useful life-skill, but it is not to have any kind of theoretical knowledge. In fact, ordinary language knows nothing of theory, and has no interest at all in achieving any sort of theoretical comprehension either of human life, or even of what **it** is that we are all **up against**.

In the new technological culture that has been developing since the mid-1950s we do perhaps begin to see some infiltration of ordinary language by theory; but otherwise ordinariness remains pretty much what it has been for several millennia. We remain up against an inscrutable **it**, sometimes benign, sometimes capricious, and sometimes desperately harsh. We love to voice our feelings in response to It, but have no expectation of and no interest in understanding it or **what it's up to**.

In ordinary language God was the human face of It, especially between about 1700 and 1914, a period when liberal Modern optimism combined with Protestant piety to produce a very friendly image of **It** as a loving heavenly Father who watched over his children and provided for their needs. The surviving God-idioms in ordinary language seem mostly to date from that period. They are these:

We are all children of God
> **God chose the best for himself** (said after tragic and premature deaths)
> **God damn it!**
> **God damn your eyes!**
> **God forbid / Heaven forbid,** or **forfend**
> **God forgive me**
> **God help him**
> **God helps those who help themselves**
> **Dear God in heaven!**
> **For God's sake!**
> **I hope to God you're right**
> **God knows! / Goodness knows**
> **God knows that /** or **how much . . .**
> **God and Mammon**
> **God moves in a mysterious way**
> **God rest his soul**
> **Godsend**
> **God speed**
> **God willing**
> And, of course, **God's gift to women,** of recent origin

Some of these idioms are – or have become – expletives and others are used in a jocular way. The way they are used often indicates that ordinary language is now as agnostic about **God** as it is about **it**. Thus **God knows!** is used to say that nobody knows, **God moves in a mysterious way** is used to say that we know nothing of why God makes things turn out as they do, and **God helps those who help themselves** – like **Praise God and keep your powder dry** – makes an ironical comment on the puritan theology by being used to say simply *Just look after* *yourself*. Not even the Puritans could really take their own theology literally. Finally, **God's gift to women** is always used ironically, to mean the opposite. Women are warned to steer well clear of him.

Thus God-talk is now very largely expletive or ironical. It no longer gives us any clear impression of what belief in God once was. For *that*, we must look to our life-idioms: they have now acquired the imaginative and religious power that the word 'God' has lost. As God fades, the **It** behind the human face of God re-emerges, and it-idioms become more numerous and vigorously expressive. Writers like Thomas Hardy and Emile Zola, novelists of **It**, become popular.

But if so, why do we not see a popular revival of classical tragedy? According to the standard story, tragedy came to a sudden end in the Enlightenment. The tragic hero, often the victim of a conflict among Powers that he cannot understand, and complaining loudly about being defeated by a harsh and incomprehensible **It**, had been merely the victim of his own ignorance. Now Newton had dispelled the old darkness, replacing **It** with a benign, humanly-intelligible cosmic order. From now on human beings can do more than just emote vainly; they can act rationally, on the basis of knowledge, to improve the human condition. Tragedy is dead because **It** is dead, being now replaced by a humanly-intelligible cosmic order and by the Design Argument, works of theodicy, and a benevolent protestant God. That wipes **It** out. During the eighteenth century even Shakespeare's tragedies were unperformable, as written. They had to be drastically edited and even rewritten to make them tolerable. Only during the nineteenth century, as the Romantic movement developed, was there a partial recovery of tragedy. Only a *partial* recovery, though, because after the rise of science and the huge growth of modern knowledge we cannot be as ignorant as the tragic hero is of the causes of suffering.

So (approximately) runs the standard account. But our investigation of **It** in ordinary language suggests that to this day the ordinary person's vision of the human lot has much in common with the world-view of classical tragedy. The main difference is that ordinary language, being 'low', is not too proud to allow itself such simple encouragements as a smile, a song and a belief in Luck. But the absorption in the struggle, the emotive-expressive use of language, and the lack of interest in theory and descriptive truth are very similar. And one may add that in all ages the protagonist, the person experiencing ruin, is apt to find explanations of his woes irritatingly irrelevant, whether they are being offered by theologians or by scientists.

Still, it is a strange conclusion to reach, that ordinary language incorporates something rather like the tragic vision. Why have we not in the twentieth century successfully demo-cratized tragic art?

To some extent, perhaps, we have: **You can't win**, says ordi-nary language; **It beats me,** mainly because I can't know why **It** has **got it in for me.** *Ours is essentially a tragic age*, says Lawrence, in the opening words of all three versions of *Lady Chatterley's Lover*: *so we refuse to take it tragically.* After a great catastrophe we don't just sit in the ruins: we begin to plan for reconstruction: *life must go on*, we say. It seems that twentieth-century attempts to make classical tragedy out of ordinary lives – Arthur Miller, Eugene O'Neill? – can scarcely avoid running into objections of one sort and another. They are undermined by the ordinary person's very 'low'-ness – his or her absurdly valiant struggle to go on, to pick up the pieces, to rebuild, and somehow keep cheerful **in spite of it all**. They are also undermined by accusations of political incorrectness, coming from those who regard optimism about the human condition and prospect as a political duty, or who demand that blame must always be pinned firmly on the *human* causes of human suffering.

These political objections have perhaps successfully inhibited a full-scale restoration of tragedy in the public culture. But ordi-nary language is not so politically-correct. It freely admits that we can easily find ourselves in a hopeless situation, where **there's not a thing we can do about it.** *That's life.*

13

The charismatic **It**

A wide range of uses of **it**, many of them already referred to, see **it** as something – usually a personal quality – that is highly specific but impossible to describe, the very thing that is needed, elusive, magical, instantly recognizable. This cluster of uses of **it** seems to begin during the later nineteenth century, and to be linked with the ideas of the avant-garde, fashion, glamour and star-quality. On the top of the tree, at the leading edge, is **where it's at. It** is something that may graciously alight upon us and stay with us for years – until suddenly we discover that we have **no longer got it.** We were **with it,** we were indeed **full of it,** even **bursting with it;** but now we have somehow **lost it.**

In short, this family of it-idioms – like a related group of life-idioms – recalls the traditional ideas of *charisma,* Grace and spirit.

The story begins in the mid-to-late nineteenth century, when **it** is *the real thing, the very thing, the genuine article,* **the absolute It, just it,** and **'That's exactly it – precisely what I had in mind'. It** is often pointed to with a demonstrative: *this,* when it is something just arriving, or a state that we are now in; and *that,* when it is something that is fully arrived and perhaps is no longer new, or is passing away.

Is this it? This is it. How long can it go on like this? Is that it? That was it. Was that it? Is that all there is to it?

These phrases strongly suggest the transfer into secular life of a strong sense of religious expectation before a holy season, the period of the feast or the re-enactment of some sacred drama, and then perhaps the sense of anti-climax when **it** is over. One pictures a young person approaching Confirmation or First

Communion (or perhaps engagement or marriage or first child-birth), who is eagerly expecting a climactic moment after which everything will be completely different – and who then perhaps reaches the point of wondering whether perhaps the great moment has already come and gone. She feels just the same: has she perhaps **missed it**?

The secular, postmodern version of all this, however, has more to do with fashion. Unexpectedly, and indeed unde-servedly, a young person finds that she is **in**. She's **got it**. **If you've got it, flaunt it. Enjoy it, make the most of it while you've got it/while it lasts.** The (usually young) person who is in this position might thirty years ago have been described as *photogenic*: now she's an *icon*. She has *star-quality, charisma*.

Such a person is a celebrity, a person who *sets* the fashion. But she or he is surrounded by a larger class of people who put a great deal of effort into being *in* the fashion, or **with it,** or **where it's at**. Such people are often called 'fans', a late nineteenth-century abbreviation of *fanatic*, another word, along with *icon, star* and *charisma*, that indicates the religious charac-ter of the whole phenomenon of Pop and celebrity culture. Graced with **it**, the star or celebrity is an emblematic person, the postmodern secular counterpart of a saint, the person everybody wants to be like.

How did this begin? Star and celebrity culture is notably classless, and evidently linked with the mass media. According to Cecil Beaton, who overstates the point, the word **It** was coined by Elinor Glyn.[20] He must mean that she took the exist-ing slang use of **it** to mean the genuine article, the very thing, the **absolute It** and transferred it to the kind of woman who might be called a *sex-goddess* or perhaps a *diva*. **It** was outstanding *sex-appeal*, and was associated with words like *allure* and *glamour*. Clara Bow became the best known **It-girl**. Men were not really supposed to have quite such a quality at all, and certainly not to be aware of possessing it: **He thinks he's it** was always said very disparagingly, as if **it** were equivalent to *the bee's knees* or *the cat's pyjamas*. **It** when ascribed to a man meant outstanding fitness for a particular post or emblematic role, or for leadership. It meant being a *high flier*, or being destined for *the top* or for great things. Thus in the first half of the twentieth century woman was still the prisoner of sex, and in her **it** always had a sexual meaning; whereas in man **it** had more to do with ideas about destiny and greatness. During the second half of the twentieth century, as the media have developed, **it** has come to be more nearly the same thing in each sex, and to be closely related to the movement of fashion. A person with **It** is a media *natural*, a starry performer whose *style* is just what the mood of the moment demands. In the jargon, the person who has got **it** is someone who is *Now*. A trendy person, a now-person.

And that *Now* is yet another item of religious vocabulary which has found a new role in contemporary culture. *Now is the day of salvation*, writes St Paul (II Cor. 6.2), and he is widely echoed in popular song: *Now is the hour*, sings Gracie Fields. Perhaps we should regard our postmodern celebrity culture as a secular return of the old cult of saints. These starry figures are our role-models; they are the people we want to be like. We see them as living in a social heaven, and we name our children after them.

14

Busily at it

Where it's at is the leading edge of fashion, a *Holy Grail* that is pursued in modern Western countries by a vast army of product designers, media people, dealers, buyers, cultural impresarios, talent-spotters and aspiring talents. There is a great deal of **money in it**. But reverse the last two words, and consider the difference between where **it's at,** and being **at it**. This being the *English* language, in which forms of words have not so much meanings as thinly-veiled implications and innuendos, a range of new and unexpected insinuations suddenly opens up.

If I am **hard at it**, it will be clear to all that I am very busily occupied in some innocent employment. (Well, I am.) If you two are **at it hammer and tongs,** you are totally absorbed in conflict. If he is **at it again**, he has resumed his old bad habits, returning like a dog to its vomit (a biblical quotation: II Peter 2.22). If someone comes upon you two **at it**, you will be engaged in sex; and if you two are **at it like knives,** the implication is that the sex in question is being performed with frantic urgency because it is more than somewhat unconventional.

Knowing ourselves to be the most plain-spoken and honest people in the entire world, we British naturally wonder how foreigners can make the absurd mistake of seeing us all as duplicitous and hypocritical rogues. It must be our language that is to blame for giving others such a false impression of what we are.

15

Leave it at that

When I was writing the life-book, I soon noticed a curious paradox. Every English speaker uses the word 'life' frequently, and
all English speakers deliver themselves of proverbs and idiomatic sayings about life. Everyone feels strongly about life; but
when challenged to say what they think the word means, almost
everyone is at a loss. Life is, er, what has departed from a
corpse: life is, er, what goes on in big cities – especially capital
cities: life is, er, sacred; it's what everybody's got a right to: Life
is, er, all this that is going on around us, and we are part of it.
Life? – well, it's obvious, isn't it?

'Life' is like 'sex', or like the verbs 'take' and 'make'. It has
accumulated such a huge range of quirky idiomatic uses that we
are no longer sure what is its 'core' or 'literal' meaning – if it has
any. We begin to suspect that ordinary language consists almost
entirely of knotted, difficult catch-phrases, stock sayings that
are batted back and forth. Native speakers use it with perfect
ease and confidence; but they themselves cannot explain it when
challenged. Ordinary language is pre-theoretical. Speakers do
not *need* to be able to understand and explain what they are
saying: all they need is the skill of using accepted forms in an
effective way.

Ordinary language is far more difficult to explain than technical professional language, and I soon found that only certain
English academics and writers could deal with the questions I
wanted to ask about the meanings of **life** today, and the history
of the meaning of **life**.

The word 'it' soon turned out to be more difficult still. **It** is
much shorter than **life, it** is not indexed to the same extent in

standard reference works, the it-idioms are harder to collect and appraise, and it quite simply doesn't have as much of 'a meaning' as life has. In the case of life I soon became confident that I could grasp the main outlines of its history. But who can write the history of it – except in the very broadest outline? As for the question What is it?, who can answer it? Often we choose to refer to something as it because we are too embarrassed or nervous or superstitious to be more explicit. We grimace, awkwardly.

In the case of life I came to a view that is fairly easy to state in six propositions:

1. We are the only beings who live in a very large and complex language-formed world of our own.

2. The basic world is the human life-world.

3. Life is the going-on of things in the human life-world.

4. Ordinary language is the principal and basic currency of the human life-world. (There are a number of others, such as music, money and mathematics, but none of them exists independently of language.)

5. During the past half-century a wide range of new idioms about life have become current in ordinary language.

6. Study of our new life-idioms reveals an emergent common religiousness of life – evidently an emergent new 'civic' religion, and a religion that is purely immanent.

Now, are we going to be able to produce a statement about it which runs parallel to this statement about life? No: not quite a *parallel* statement. The logic of it is not like the logic of life. In the case of it, propositions 1–4 may be allowed to stand, and then we will begin to diverge.

We will say, first (5), that ordinary language is very largely, and almost entirely phatic; that is, it is used not to report facts – it seems actively to dislike being specific – but to express our feelings, and for purposes of social interaction. Our utterances are passwords, speech-acts, moves in various 'situations' or language-games. But it seems (6), that the human life-world does not consist solely of a web or net of communication, with messages flying back and forth. For the content of the messages

itself attests the presence *and the constraining influence* not only
of senders and receivers, personal pronouns, but also of a background something that is pervasive and impersonal – or, at any
rate, ungendered. This Other does not appear directly, but is
indicated by the idiomatic uses of the third-person singular
neuter pronoun It. When it is something particular and finite, it
may be any matter, business, concern or thing that a person has
to contend with. But there does arise in the idioms a strong
tendency to see all of human life as a struggle against it. Because
ordinary language is so strongly phatic, it remains largely or
wholly unspecified and nameless. For one reason and another,
it can't be talked about directly. It is kept veiled. So it tends to
become the unmentionable, the unspeakable, the indescribable
and the ineffable. (As we will shortly discover, in 21 below, it
may also be the unavowable.) It therefore attracts the range
of emotions associated with whatever is nameless – disgust,
horror, anxiety, sublimity, sacred awe. It may loom so large that
it threatens to over-master and destroy us. Life begins to look
like a battle to maintain one's morale and one's will-to-live in
the face of It-all.

Comforters seek in various ways to support those who are
letting it get them down. But, and very strikingly, many philosophical and religious systems of thought offer representations
of it that, it is hoped, will make it easier to deal with.

Thus the hero-cults of antiquity portrayed It as a monster
which is slain by a hero. This theme returns vividly in modern
SF books and films, in many of which the monster has indeed
been designated It.

It may be pictured as Destiny, Fate or determining Necessity.
Here ancient philosophy often suggested that by going along
with what must be, and even willing it for oneself, one can
attain a certain freedom. And perhaps this theme also returns in
modern popular culture, as a way of coping with either genetic
or psychological determinism. Instead of vainly attempting to
change or hide our true nature, we should with 'pride' come out
and affirm it.

Again, It may be represented as the Will of God. Ideas of God

seek to show that **It is not as bad as we feared.** In early times
God was as fearsome and erratic as **It**; but God gradually
becomes more loving and merciful. The picture of God as personal suggests the possibility of some sort of negotiation with
God in prayer. The believer starts to talk, saying at first things
like **Let it not be so** and **May it not happen;** but through the
struggle she/he gradually comes to the point of being able to say
Amen, **So be it, Let it be.** Thus prayer looks like a way of
reconciling oneself to It.

Ordinary language contains traces of all these approaches,
and more. Perhaps it must treat each and all of them as being
no more than putatively-'helpful' myths, because it – that is,
ordinary language – is phatic and therefore agnostic about such
matters. Ordinary language does not supply any identifying
description of **it**, so there isn't literally any such thing as **telling
it like it is,** or **making it plain,** or **getting it right,** or **doing it
justice.**

I have elsewhere suggested that the entire modern human life-
world may be regarded as a secularization of the old sacred
world of religion. In which case we might be able to see **it**
as being the postmodern counterpart of the awkward member
of the ancient pantheon: that is, a figure such as Loki in
Scandinavian mythology, or the Adversary (Hebrew: Satan) in
Yahweh's heavenly court. This character is like God's **Id** or dark
side, but he has at least one great function: he starts the plot.
Even in the perfect world there is a touch of incompleteness,
awkwardness, grit; a possibility of things going wrong. If it were
not so there would be no story to tell.

So perhaps **It** returns in postmodernity to remind us that
perfection is never fully achieved: **We can't have it all our own
way: it is as if it has a mind of its own; it** seems to represent
something as enduring, obdurate and resistant as a camel.

Taking it all in

If you doubt what I say about how knotted and idiosyncratic ordinary language is, consider the following sixteen ways of **taking it:**

take it that (proceed upon the assumption that . . .)
take it in (understand)
take it up (a task, a cause)
take it out (destroy)
take it out on (expend one's wrath upon . . .)
take it over (assume control)
take it away! (play on, maestro!)
take it easy
take it on the chin
take it like a man
take it from here
take it from me
take it or leave it
take it for granted
take it as read
take it to the limit

Redeeming it all

After his death in the First World War his widow Helen Thomas published two short *novellae* about her life with Edward Thomas, the poet. The first she titled **As it Was** (1926),[21] with a double meaning. The story promises to be a truthful record of events just as they happened: this is my testimony, this story must now be told, and **this is how it was**. But in the same words she is echoing the *Gloria Patris: As it was in the beginning*. The suggestion that she makes here is quite complex: religious myth around the world claims that there was an age of gold at the beginning of the world when **It**, or **It-all**, the whole set-up, was perfectly happy and blessed. The *Gloria Patris* seems to say that in worship we contact a realm or a level on which that perfection has not been wholly lost, but endures. And Helen Thomas's title suggests that she has had her own personal Eden, now lost. By fixing **it** in writing she's doing what a human being can do to ensure that **it** too is now and ever shall be.

The second story, *World without End* (1931) repeats the theme: 'world without end' means 'for the rest of time, for as long as the world remains unended'. Helen Thomas is putting down the facts about something that she had for a few years, the one thing above all else that **makes it all worthwhile**, and she is saying that this is her testimony; **let it stand** till the end of time. So she fixes an **it** that is at once factual, sacred and undying.

It does of course very often happen that when some notable figure dies his surviving relatives make great efforts to gather and guard all his remains, and especially his letters. They keep his study and his archive untouched, with **everything just as it was**. In extreme cases they almost *mummify* him, his remains and his reputation, excluding all outsiders and especially biographers.

Helen Thomas does not make this common mistake. She certainly does not **tell only the best of it**. Nor does she try to **make the best of it**. On the contrary, she has promised to **get it right**. She **makes it clear** that their circumstances were almost always difficult and often very meagre. Thomas hardly ever had any very regular employment, and was often away. In fact, by today's standards at least, he was pretty impossible. He did not lack the customary faults of poets and other creative persons: he could appear vain, self-absorbed, depressive and neglectful. But though **she does not conceal it**, she does not in the least **hold it against him**. At the end one realises with sudden surprise that Helen Thomas has not justified herself – on the contrary, she pictures herself as a bit of a doormat, too lacking in confidence and too clinging – and she hasn't justified her husband. Nor is she suggesting that theirs was a great love and a perfect marriage. What she has done is to have told the story in a way that has redeemed **it**. Love and memory and a rather artless art have successfully transformed the transient **it** of life into something like *Heilsgeschichte*, salvation history, a story that **makes it all worthwhile**.

Many religious people believe that if each individual person were to be saved, or redeemed, the world would instantly be a better place. Many politically-motivated people have supposed that if the human political set-up were to be put right, the world would very soon be a better place. Both groups of people are obviously mistaken. But Helen Thomas prompts a new and curious thought: the *unum necessarium*, the 'one thing needful', is the redemption not of me, nor of you, nor of us all, but of **it**.

And this in turn suggests a new way of identifying **it**. Perhaps **it** is not the Joker, and not Satan, but what Leibniz calls 'metaphysical evil'?[22]. By 'metaphysical evil' is meant finitude, transience, death and all the various limits that have been thought to blight our life and make it impossible for human beings ever to be fully content with our life here 'below', **just as it is**. From inside language we feel the pressure of what seems to be an 'external' constraint, like a corset. Many people may prefer to describe this constrainer as 'objective reality', or 'matter'; but I am suggesting that in philosophy it might be called finitude, or metaphysical evil.

Helen Thomas's story is told in a way that brings out all the limitations – including the big one, Death, which overhangs the whole of both books – but also overcomes them. The way she writes says Yes to **It all**, and so redeems **It. It has all been worthwhile**.

Amongst animals the species is more important than the individual, and so long as the species survives there does not usually need to be any record of the individual life. But amongst humans the need to find a way to **make It All worthwhile** is fundamental. We have to do it: we mark graves, recall genealogies, compose and preserve epitaphs, obituaries, letters, diaries and memoirs, and keep annals, registers and records. By thus encoding the transient flux of life into signs we hope to invest it with meaning.

18

It as an ordeal

A number of It-idioms seem to picture **it** as an ordeal, a period of severe stress and pain imposed upon someone as a test of character. **There's no choice about it.** You must **stick it out.** You must simply **put up with it,** and **see it through** or **go through with it,** the word 'through' suggesting something like a passage through fire or water, as in *The Magic Flute.* When you recognize an ordeal for what it is, you know that it is inappropriate to complain. Complaints may be met with grim retorts such as **If you don't like it then you must lump it,** or **You haven't seen the half of it yet.** Later, you may hear the more encouraging **The worst of it is over now,** and you know that you have almost come to **the end of it.** Finally, **It's all over.**

These idioms may be said to show how it-talk deals with the problem of evil, and in particular the problem of unmerited suffering. We don't claim any personal knowledge of or communion with **It,** and we can't suppose that **it** has personal qualities or is in any way predisposed in favour of human beings. Nor is **it** going to become any friendlier in the future. **It is what it is.** So when a period of severe suffering and stress begins, the most rational policy is to treat it as an ordeal, by enduring which without complaint we can be purged and hardened. **Put it down to experience,** as they say. **Learn from it.**

19

Can ordinariness ever understand itself?

In section 15, above, I was suggesting that ordinary language is pretheoretical and not at all concerned with developing an accurate map of the world. On the contrary, it consists very largely of 'knotted, difficult catchphrases, stock sayings that are batted back and forth' for purposes of social interaction. Such language, as in banter, effectively creates complicity and establishes common feelings, but it is not being used descriptively. Consider how language is used on packaging: when just about everything is being called *pure, fresh, natural, tingling, country* and *farmhouse* language is not being used to create understanding or to give information. Consider the rapid succession of new words invented by the young to express commendation: *fab, brill, wicked, evil* and others come into use and pass away, not in a restless search for more precise descriptive terms, but because the leading edge of common feeling, **where it's at**, moves and must move all the time. We are not talking about rapidly-changing facts, but about the use of rapidly-changing *passwords*.

Native speakers, we said earlier, *use* the curiously-difficult stock phrases of ordinary language with perfect ease and confidence, but they don't need to be able to *understand* what they are saying: all they need is the skill of fencing – making the currently-prescribed moves at high speed, so as to show that one can *keep up* with others. The keeping-up is **what it's all about**, because ordinary language is about *belonging*.

It is also about giving reassurance. Imagine that you are one of a small party of travellers, walking towards a village or climbing a hill. From time to time the younger members of the group ask what may seem to be a factual question such as *How much further is it?*, *When will we get there?* and *Are we going the right way?* You may yourself put the same questions to a native person whom you meet on the way. But such questions are never answered factually. Everywhere, around the world, ordinary language considers it polite to return the reassuring answer that the questioner is understood to seek: *We won't be long now, nearly there, just a bit further, not far now.*

Ordinary language knows almost nothing of fact-stating or of theory. It is often very clever and fast, and it just *loves* irony, but it cares nothing for reflection. It is full of theoretical inconsistencies, but it doesn't worry about them in the least.

One of the most notable areas of inconsistency has already figured prominently in the present discussion. Ordinary language in its movement back and forth shows that the process of events in the human life-world does not run unconstrained. On the contrary, it continually shows itself feeling external constraint or pressure. So strongly is this felt that in ancient literature one of the most pervasive images of human life pictures it as a battle against a monster, or as a struggle to escape from a Fate that nevertheless keeps pursuing us and must one day catch up with us.

What is this non-human thing that presses upon us and requires us to confront it? The vocabulary in which we acknowledge it is very large and untidy: Fate, Necessity, Destiny, Fortune, God, It, It-all, Things, Everything, the Other, Death, Finitude and more. This very large vocabulary has been historically-accumulated over many centuries, and indeed millennia. In recent times the word it has perhaps become the most favoured term of all. But ordinary language has no special interest in tidying itself up, or in systematizing its world-view. So we continue to use a variety of phrases that are relics of a number of different world-views.

This picturesque confusion prevails widely. Suppose, for example, someone says: 'I'm in low spirits. I can't think what's got into me. Perhaps I should go back on those pills?' In these three sentences the speaker uses language that evokes theories from very different epochs in the history of medicine: Galen's theory of humours, ideas of possession, and our own contemporary brain-chemistry-and-pills approach to psychological problems. But ordinary language doesn't mind a bit. It doesn't even *notice* the apparent inconsistency. It doesn't care in the least about theory. All it is interested in is vivid, punchy phrases that voice feelings, do their jobs, and successfully transact the chief business of everyday life – which is 'networking' with other people.

Now we can put the question: Can ordinariness understand itself? Answer: no, for ordinariness is pre-theoretical. It has no *interest* in understanding itself. It doesn't need to have theories about how it works. It just is, and knows only that it works. Its use *shows* that it works. It is the heart and core of all language, everywhere presupposed; and the various specialized vocabularies in which we build our various sciences, theories, systems of belief and pictures of the world are related to it as its 'outshuts' are to an old vernacular longhouse, extensions that are both supported by and supporting it.

Ordinariness, then, cannot understand itself, and has no interest in understanding itself. It just is, and knows that it works. But now: can understanding understand ordinariness? No, not altogether, because in our tradition understanding has always been all about *escaping* from ordinariness, rather than trying to comprehend it. Even a smidgen of education leads people to look down upon those who are, and upon all that is, merely ordinary. Understanding has always seen ordinariness as being low and comical because it is unaware of itself. So in our theatre ordinary people have been comic characters since the late Middle Ages, and still are.

Since Plato there has been in our culture an important contrast between two groups of people, the wise and the vulgar. The vulgar are the common people who use the vulgar tongue, the vernacular. (In Latin, *vulgus* means 'the common people'.) So the vulgar are ordinary people, whose life is lived simply within the world of ordinary language. They live inside Plato's Cave. The wise, by contrast, are that very small group of people who by education have been lifted up out of ordinariness into the brightly-lit higher world of theory. (In Greek, *theoria* means seeing, vision, contemplation.)

Since Plato, virtually our whole tradition has drawn a sharp distinction between the twilit regions inhabited by ordinary people and ordinary language, and the clear light of theoretical understanding in which dwell the wise who have been enlightened by education. Thus for Plato the contrast between networking and knowledge is a contrast between darkness and light, confusion and clarity. Both in Plato and in much Asian thought it seemed obvious that the small enlightened group should either govern, or at least supply the King with his counsellors and ministers. And it seemed appropriate that one should distinguish between two levels of truth: a conventional, mythical sort of truth for the vulgar, and a higher, more conscious and purely philosophical kind of truth known only to the wise.

Inevitably, this whole system of thought seemed entirely to separate the world of what can be clearly understood from the world of ordinary language and ordinary people. But equally inevitably, the rise of political democracy and mass higher education was bound to bring it all to an end. The relation between ordinariness and our various systems of knowledge and forms of theoretical understanding has now to be entirely rethought.

Hence my analogy of an old vernacular longhouse and the various additions made to it over the past four centuries.[23]

Originally, the rectangular house was divided into just two rooms, an open hall and a parlour, separated only by a light wooden screen, a cross-passage and a central hearth below a hole in the roof. The life of the household was highly communal. There were no separate service rooms, and all the functions of life were performed publicly, in common space, except perhaps for the fact that the master and mistress might retire to the parlour behind the screen to sleep privately.

Individualism and a demand for greater safety and privacy

brought about the first change. A big central chimney stack was built. It incorporated a baking oven, and a staircase wound round the side of it, leading up to bedrooms on a newly-constructed upper floor.

In later years various outshuts were added. One housed a dairy, with stone shelves. Others might house a kitchen, and a pantry. Even the dog might move out into a small doghouse, also in the form of a lean-to outshut. And these various outshuts provided for the more efficient performance of various special functions. By the early twentieth century the old farmhouse might have grown to four or five times its original size. But the same two rooms were still the meeting place and the heart of the house, to which all the other and more recent spaces referred back. And so it remains to this day.

This analogy suggests that the old highly élitist, and indeed 'classist' type of philosophy was a mistake. It drastically de-valorized ordinariness, and it over-valued theoretical under-standing and objective knowledge. It wrongly supposed that the higher type of human being, whether contemplative religious or philosopher or scientist, could become and had become com-pletely detached from the ordinariness that uses language just for networking – sharing feelings and interacting socially with others. The result was that ordinariness seemed to be low, comical and unworthy of serious attention. Indeed, it was strictly unintelligible, because there was nothing in it to be understood; and in a class society the wise and the vulgar lived in carefully-separated worlds. They didn't, and couldn't, com-mune with each other. High culture was thought to be entirely different from folk or popular culture.

I am suggesting, though, that the arrival of political demo-cracy and mass higher education displaces the old dualism. Nowadays *most* of the vulgar are learning to add on their own personal outshuts of specialist knowledge, theoretical under-standing and technical skill. The average person is getting to look like my old vernacular farmhouse, which has been modified and extended to keep up with social and technological change, but which happily remains premodern at its core. And it's about time that the wise learnt to understand ordinariness, because in fact they themselves are not and never could be as wholly emancipated from it as they purported to be. And I have been suggesting that ordinariness is in any case very much more complex and surprising than the wise have supposed. Indeed, ordinariness is an unknown world that we are only just beginning to explore. It is, in truth, very much more difficult to keep up with the gossip, the banter, the teasing, the irony and the dark hints that are flying around in the hall than it is to follow the simple technical instructions that guide what is done in the dairy or the workshop.

Ordinariness may be complex and unsystematic, but it does supply people with extensive – and much-needed – resources for coping with the ups and down of life. This raises the question of whether the wise, with their own rationally-worked-out procedures and systems of thought, are in practice really any better off than the vulgar. In the life-book we produced and examined the 100–150 newish idioms about life that are now established in ordinary language, and then asked the question: Is the ordinary person, equipped with and guided by these idioms, better or less well able to cope with life than the person who has a systematically-worked out theology or philosophy to live by? And we found that the ordinary person, who has only the idioms current in ordinary language to live by, comes out of the comparison rather well. Despite Plato, it is not clear that the wise do any better than the ordinariness they have so long despised.

The same may be said in relation to the subject-matter of this present book. Suppose we ask: What ultimately governs and limits our life and our several fates? Is it Necessity, or just Chance, or is it God, or perhaps in these agnostic times plain old unspecific It? The wise have inherited from Plato the belief that there is and has to be just one true theory of the world; so they must select, develop and commit themselves to just one theory, be it Determinism or Libertarianism, Realism, Idealism or Theism, or whatever. But amongst the wise we find, first that all the seats get taken, because every position in philosophy gets occupied by someone or other; and secondly, that the debate between the different theories of the world is never quite finally resolved. So the wise are divided amongst themselves forever; and, whatever the truth may be, most of the wise must be badly wrong.

Ordinary language, on the other hand, recognizes the interpretative plasticity of the world. **It all depends on how you look at it.** So ordinary language is content to be eclectic, and has idioms related to all the principal theories. But ordinary language is not static, and I have suggested that since the 1870s there has been a significant shift towards the it-idioms, and towards something like the Huxleyan image of life as a chess game played against an enigmatic, patient, invisible opponent who evades the Turing Test and keeps us guessing forever. But **It** has many faces and may attract a wide range of feelings, and I am led to conclude (i) that we in our age need to pay more attention to ordinariness – which means, in effect, ordinary language – than was given to it in the past; (ii) that the philosophical and religious outlook embodied in ordinary language is subtler than it is given credit for; and (iii) that ordinariness belongs to us all, is more coherent, and offers a better starting-point for future thought than the endless and unresolved controversies of the wise.

20

Books about It

Why is **it** so scarce in book titles? It-monsters are found in E. Nesbit, **Five Children and It** (1903) and Stephen King, **IT** (1986). In a few other books It is the complex of comic or tragic tensions, understandings and misunderstandings that there may be between men and women: William Shakespeare, **As You Like It**; Helen Thomas, **As it Was** (1926); and Julian Barnes, **Talking about It** (1991). But where are the rest? On the Internet, I found that US *Amazon* listed 14816 titles incorporating the word **it**, but they were almost without exception titles of the do-it-yourself and how-it-works type, and not of great literary interest.

By contrast, film titles yielded a very rich harvest. About 40 films have a title that begins with the word **It**, 327 films include the word, and a further 20 have **it** in their alternative titles. In about half of all these cases the whole title is, or has created, an established it-idiom.

Why the difference? Perhaps film-titles are, and have to be, more colloquial. It-idioms generally are much more prominent in the spoken language than the written, presumably because in the colloquy-situation the persons gathered together will as a matter of courtesy wish to speak to each other in a way that avoids any acknowledgement of external and non-human threats or pressures limiting the ease and freedom of their speech. **Not a bit of it!**, they exclaim, because for us who are here now, we are all there is. It-idioms courteously set aside matters that might be distracting or disagreeable. Their use in film-titles, then, acts as a come-hither, an invitation to intimacy and a promise of revelations. What is more, from early times a film-show was *itself* a faintly conspiratorial social gathering of a voyeuristic kind. So film is a medium that likes to use gossipy and suggestive it-idioms.

21

Leaving it unsaid: the *unavowable*

In section 5 we discussed the various ways in which it cannot be put into more explicit words, because it is either *unmentionable* (rather improper, or embarrassing), or *unspeakable* (violently disgusting and shocking), or *unnameable* (horrifying, or monstrous), or *indescribable* (sublime, perhaps), or *ineffable* (a sacred mystery). But there is also another it that cannot be verbalized because **it is best left unsaid** – and in any case one may be very unsure **what it amounts to**. It is the *unavowable* or *undeclarable*, because to **avow it** would at once change the whole situation drastically and irreversibly. When one **avows it** one takes *one's life in one's hands*, because in that situation 'There! I've said it' means 'I've done it'. Indeed, I'm probably done *for*.

About this **it** one may have strong suspicions, and voicing them may have far-reaching consequences: yet it may not be there at all. There may be **nothing in it** (or, interestingly, **nothing to it**), and the suspicions may be quite baseless or groundless. In which case one should *hold one's tongue* and not voice one's suspicions, because one may be *stirring up trouble, making a mountain out of a molehill* and causing *much ado about nothing*. **It's best** to say **I don't want to talk about it**, and *steer clear* of the whole subject.

In a case of this kind **it** is actually brought into being by uttering it. So long as **it** remains unvoiced, no harm is done. *Least said, soonest mended.* But as soon as **it** is *avowed*, **it** is *there*: indeed, our very use of the formal terms *avow* and *declare*, rather than a simpler word like *confess* or *admit*, shows that we are conscious that the declaration creates a new situation. It is a performative utterance. From now on, and **like it or not**, there is indeed *something between them*. For I have in mind, of course, some such case as this: A appears (to others, and perhaps also to A) to be half in love with B. B, half-suspecting this, seems (to others, and perhaps also to B) to be on the point of falling in love with A. And C, who has a strong interest in the matter, suspects that there may be *something between them*, or even (putting it a bit more strongly) that there may be *some kind of understanding* – presumably tacit – between them. However, the actual situation is by no means as cut and dried as I have suggested, because each party can see it only from her or his own viewpoint, which is itself highly uncertain. There is no omniscient observer, who knows what – if anything – is really going on. Everyone's just guessing. A, B and C may each of them wonder privately: 'Am I **just imagining it?**' And this raises a further doubt, because **imagining it** can't help but get entangled with the roving *fancy* that speculatively eyes various possible objects to see whether they *tickle* it. In these matters, everyone speculates, most flirt a little and convention holds that nothing has happened, *no harm has been done* and there's **nothing to it** until the *fateful* moment when someone **says it**, and thereby **brings it out into the open.**

In this case, what is now out in the open did not previously exist in the dark, where it should have been kept. Before the fateful words that made it explicit, it was no more than a speculative possibility, a surmise, a guess, a fancy, a suspicion. **It had crossed my mind,** as people say, but only as an hypothesis; whereas now the issue has been forced. There will doubtless have to be various highly-embarrassed protestations and denials, at length, and afterwards, much discomfort.

This example of the way spoken utterances crystallize situations, and *move the action on a stage* in everyday life brings out clearly the close affinity between 'ordinariness' and the theatre. A philosopher who goes to the theatre starts wondering what dramatic action *is* – a topic that has not been discussed as much as it deserves. Our example supplies us with an illuminating case, where in a small circle of people speculations, fancies, sus-

picions build up. It's all very nebulous, so uncertain that nobody
is quite sure that **there is anything in it**. We describe everyone's
preoccupation as **it** because it would be wrong to *spell out* our
suspicions prematurely. **It** is what, for the present at least, is **best
left unsaid**. But the tension builds up, until somebody makes a
sudden move that **lets it out** and **gives it away**: a short explosion
of jealousy, or an unmistakeable sign, or perhaps a nervous but
determined avowal. Then, **it's out**, a new situation has come
into being, and everyone must take up a fresh position. And we
have here an excellent example of how the action is moved on
a stage, both in ordinary life and in the theatre. There is, in life
and theatre, an interplay between the implicit and the explicit,
freedom and commitment, fidelity and infidelity, the open and
the doubtful. There are periods of dreaming enchantment, and
moments when a single utterance breaks the spell and suddenly
forces change. And we use the word **it** to refer to something
looming up that is, for the moment at least, best left unsaid.
Best to say nowt about it, they said when I was young: **Leave it
be. Leave it alone. Come off it. Drop it. Give it a rest. Cut it out.
It ain't necessarily so.**

22

Do we really need it?

I have argued elsewhere that the ideas of the self and the world are correlated. There cannot be a self without a world, which needs to include at least some other selves, and in which the self can function as a self; and there cannot be a world without at least one self whose world it is. The world is at least the self's necessary arena, and the self is the world's necessary voice that forms it, structures it, brightens it, makes it intelligible and knows it as world.

However, in religion, in utopian politics and in philosophy there is a widespread suggestion that the True World, the perfect world, will consist *only* of selves, friendly, equal and fully reconciled to each other. Thus in Christian art, and in many other traditions, the heavenly world may be portrayed simply as a large crowd of shining beings who look very much alike. Presumably the angels are made to look like clones by way of indicating that there can be no discord amongst them. Idealist philosophers such as Hegel, McTaggart and Macmurray have similarly pictured the perfect world as a perfect society. And in politics, various anarchists and Marxists have claimed that such a society was realizable, and would soon come on this earth.

Now you may say that all these dreams are historically indebted to a single source, namely ancient Jewish eschatology, with its promise of a final victory over the powers of evil and a messianic age of ease and plenty. With the rise of science and the fading of religious utopianism as an imaginative and political force, the old millenarian dreams will surely fade. Not so: for surely the tendency of our present argument has been to say that ordinary language battles to get as near as it can to the very same view. Personalistic pluralism – the doctrine that 'the Real' consists ultimately of a society of finite selves – is pretty well entrenched, both in the way we use ordinary language and in the ordinary person's vision of the world. This is true especially of young persons, city-dwellers, and 'the top ten thousand' persons who used to be described collectively as 'Society'. Their way of life, which consisted of an endless series of meetings with each other, was generally accepted as being the most privileged form of life.

Consider the extent to which in Shakespeare's theatrical world every character and every play is interested in one thing and one thing only: the world of human social relationships. Language is used simply by way of contributing to the business of that world. The external physical world, so far as it is acknowledged *at all*, is treated simply as supplying a stock of useful metaphors. Drama is like that because people are like that, and ordinary language is like that. So is the novel, very largely: hence epistolary and conversational novels, and Alice's opinion that to be interesting a book must have plenty of conversations in it. For normal persons, socializing is the chief end of human life, and I have throughout the present discussion been uneasily considering the hypothesis that the reason for most it-talk is merely that ordinary people and ordinary language habitually cut to the minimum any time-wasting reference to the non-human world around us. The word 'it' briefly alludes to the non-human – and dismisses it. It is an irritating distraction: **we don't need it, so let's say no more about it.** When we are chatting together we like to talk as if there is no **it**, and only *we* exist. Nothing is more important than gatherings such as this, of us, now.

Is **it**-talk then no more than a dismissive and minimal acknowledgement of the ambient non-human world? **Do we really need it?** Could we be **rid of it** altogether? Surely all our utopian dreams, whether religious or political, are dreams of a human world without any **it**? Don't we associate **it** with everything that we would prefer to put out of our minds: the pressure of necessity, fate, destiny; the vicissitudes of luck, fortune, chance, contingency; life's lurking background of evil, death, nothingness; and a fear that It-All, encircling us, is rather more demanding, or rather colder, than we want to know? Perhaps then when we gather close for a gossip, our it-talk functions both to acknowledge the surrounding darkness and to keep it at bay? For a while, the demons are fended off and we inhabit an ideal, convivial humans-only world.

That word *gossip*, as everyone knows, can be used either of the flow of talk or of any person who loves to gossip. Before that it meant one's own close friend, a person with whom one loves to talk, for a *God-sib* is a godparent, a baptismal sponsor to whom one is close kin 'spiritually' or 'in God'. So gossip, just *gossip*, literally expresses communion in God, and ordinary language does see in the intimate talk of close friends an image of an ideal spiritual world.

A world, that is, with no **it** – but, notoriously, a negation is also a reminder. The light and inexplicit little word **it**, with which all talk is peppered, cannot help but convey a whispered reminder of **it** as the *unmentionable* (the improper and indecent), **it** as the *unspeakable* (the disgusting and nauseating), **it** as the *unnameable* (the 'horrible' and terrifying), **it** as the *indescribable* (the sublime and awe-inspiring), and **it** as the *ineffable* (an awesome, sacred mystery).[24] That is to say, the very moves by which we seek to exclude something and dismiss **it** from our minds cannot help but also re-mind us of **it**. So the moves by which we switch on the lights, draw the curtains and gather close together serve also to heighten the contrast between our own little circle and the surrounding dark.

In the same way, when one is in good society, one's talk must be *light*. One must **make light of it**: that is, there must be no reference to evil, hardship, bad news, limitation, pressure, conflict or even the need to work. Indeed, one could almost define **it** as comprising all the topics that one must not refer to when in Society. If in your innocence you skirt or even broach one of them, you will be instantly pooh-poohed. Your wrist will be tapped. No, no: you mustn't talk of such unpleasant topics. **That's it. It won't do**: we go to some lengths to exclude **it**. But **it's there**, nevertheless. In one way and another, **it makes itself** felt. Like sin, it 'couches at the door'.[25] Eventually, one will have to **deal with it.**

23

What's It All about?

It-talk has a way of 'going cosmic', and the moment when it does so is the moment when the speaker starts using the phrase **it all** instead of the shorter and simpler **it**. One typical situation – already discussed in 9 above – arises where **it** is the business with which we are presently engaged – a course of life, a project, a task, an employment, a responsibility, an obsession, a compulsion, a vocation. Everything goes swimmingly so long as we feel that we **have it under control**, but come the day when we find **it getting out of hand**, and we'll be heard making the switch to **It All**:

> It's all a bit too much
> It's all going horribly wrong
> What's the point of it all?
> I can't take it all in
> Can you see any point behind it all?
> Where will it all end?
> What does it all mean?
> You need to get away from it all

and so on: the number of idioms available to us at this point is very large. They mark a point at which ordinary language goes proto-philosophical. The person who complains about **It All** is asking for some form of *cognitive therapy* – or perhaps for faith (which may be much the same thing). What is needed is an over-all rationale or rationalization of the situation through which the troubled one will be able to **get things into perspective**, and *get his life back*. We are talking about a confidence in life (confidence = full trust), and an ability to manage one's own life, which one is hardly aware of needing and having until one finds that it has suddenly and unexpectedly failed. And it is at this point of doubt and despair about **it all** that people are most receptive to the influence of religion.

More subtle and complex is the line of thought that we were opening up in section 22, and earlier. Ordinary language, evolved to be the currency in which the daily business of social life is transacted, likes to posit a purely-human world like the worlds of the theatre, of heaven, of 'the stars' and of 'Society'. But around the brightly-lit stage of ordinary social life there is a large penumbra of things that are indecent and *ought not* to be talked about; things that are not nice but unpleasant, and which we would *prefer not* to talk about; and things that are somehow beyond language and *cannot* be talked out. The word **it** does not have a meaning, being merely a neuter pronoun, so that it is conveniently used as a colourless euphemism that alludes to the Other, while keeping it at a certain distance, and out of direct view. However, our it-idioms are very numerous and very striking, and they cannot help but become emotionally coloured by the Other that they veil. Inevitably, they keep reminding us of the very things that they were meant to hide – fate and fortune, God, contingency, death, evil and nothingness, and all that lurks beneath the polished surface of both individual and social life. Here, when we speak of **It All**, rather than simply **It**, we express our sense of how completely, and in how many ways, the human life-world is encircled by **it**.

Interestingly, the metaphors in which ordinary language speaks of our managing or coping with life still evoke the old task of managing a working animal such as an ox or a camel; and the metaphors in which ordinary language speaks about **it** still evoke the picture of a circle of human beings around a blazing fire who are, for the moment, happy in the knowledge that the various lurking creatures of the night are being kept at a safe distance. Whether it's a matter of being able to domesticate and control a horse or of being able to defend yourself against a dangerous animal, the whole business of being able to cope with animals remains to this day a very powerful metaphor for self-control, for the ability to cope with life, and for social control.[26]

Is there also a blessed **It-All**, which is not something that is to be excluded from private conversation, nor to be feared or complained about or wrestled with, but on the contrary is to be envied and admired? What about the person who **has it all** – that is, **it** in the sense of youth, talent, charisma, beauty and good fortune?

Notice the difference between **having it all** and **having everything**. **The man who has everything** is the man for whom it is hard to choose a present because he is so rich and already has so many possessions, whereas the girl who **has it all** has all the enviable things that *cannot* be purchased. Merely being rich is not interesting, but the **it**-gifts are out of the common human run. The person who has them is always thought of as having been specially favoured by the gods in a way that reminds us all too vividly how utterly arbitrary is the gods' distribution of their favours, and so provokes violent feelings. The person who **has it all** often needs protection. She's *besieged* by a pack of admirers who are not very far from becoming a lynch mob. She is envied, stalked and bitterly resented. The people who try to get near her know that wealth and possessions, mere **everything**, can easily be shared around; but the **it**-gifts cannot. If you try to get near someone who has them, all you gain is a painful reminder of life's incomprehensible unfairness. And in addition, the people who **have it all** themselves often have a bad time. One might say that just as the average person sometimes **finds it all a bit too much,** so the exceptional person may also find that **having it all** is *also* **a bit too much**, and wish that she had instead been just average. Complaints along these lines are familiar to readers of, for example, Kierkegaard and Wittgenstein – and I don't doubt their sincerity.

So **it** is always something ambivalent, anomalous and extrahuman, something difficult to handle and difficult to talk clearly about; and even if **It's a blessing**, then it is often a very *mixed* blessing. The case of personal charisma, on the bright side of life, is not so very different from the case of the various 'ultimates' and other bogies, on the dark side of life.

After these preliminaries, we are now ready to return to the opening question: **What is it all about?** We have earlier suggested that in ordinary language the sudden change from **it** to **it all** marks the point at which **it**-talk goes cosmic, a point at which people may be receptive to metaphysical or religious ideas. But an important difference is to be noted: it seems that our it-idioms operate in a rather archaic region which does not yet distinguish between the good and the evil supernatural.

The point here is of great consequence. Christian societies – and perhaps especially, Protestant societies like the USA – are usually seen as having a dualistic world-view, in accordance with the Faith's apocalyptic origins. The world is divided up pretty sharply between the good guys and the bad guys, the permitted and the forbidden, the righteous and the sinners. It is important to 'test the spirits', to search one's conscience, and to be confident that one is indeed amongst the elect. Today's political correctness is a continuation of Protestantism by other means.

Ordinary language, however, and at least in Britain, does not support this vision of the world. Its basic contrast is not that between the empires of God and Satan, the righteous and the reprobate sinners: on the contrary, its basic world-view appears to be radical humanism surrounded by bad dreams, many of them left over from its pagan, as well as its Christian, past. The world *is* the conversation of humanity – a conversation that is carried on in the home, the street, the shop, the workshop, the courtroom and the debating chamber: a conversation in which the recurrent little word **it** is a reminder and a symptom of all that has been and is being tacitly excluded for the moment, so that the conversation which everyone is enjoying so much may continue without being interrupted by a jarring false note.

The conversation functions as a tacit conspiracy to keep the bad dreams out of mind. A few people are haunted by them, people who find parties difficult; intellectuals, like the prophet Jeremiah. **It All** got him down:

I did not sit in the company of the merrymakers,
        nor did I rejoice;
I sat alone, because thy hand was upon me,
        for thou hadst filled me with indignation.
Why is my pain unceasing,
        my wound incurable,
        refusing to be healed?
Wilt thou be to me like a deceitful brook,
        like waters that fail?

Jeremiah 15.17f.

The world-view of ordinary language is, I am suggesting, a cheerful, low and unmoralistic radical humanism which, nevertheless, bears traces of many old bad dreams of an encircling nonhuman outside. Most people can keep **it** at bay, most of the time. But sometimes **It all becomes too much.** Then people turn to religion, to philosophy, or to the more recent (and much less ambitious) therapies offered by science. Ordinary language, though, prefers to go on offering its own rough consolations, as if confident that 'Malt does more than Milton can / To justify God's ways to man'. **Don't let it get you down:** friendship, courage, cheerfulness and dogged endurance will get you through **it all** – and **if you don't like it you'll just have to lump it.**

Notice this curiosity: **Keep it up!** – and then, less cheerfully, **It's all up with me.** Isn't ordinary language a puzzle?

24

Taking life as it comes

Still the question persists: what in ordinary language is the relationship between *life* and *it*? By 'life' we mean the flowing human life-world which is nowadays in effect the religious object, in which we live and move and have our being, and which fills and vitalizes us. So is it a part of life, or is it life's Other, and almost *opposite*?

I suggest that life is not an infinite but a *finite* religious object, and that it is hinted at, alluded to, and somehow *felt* along life's boundary. Again I say: just look at a series of it-idioms and see once again how very dark and unspecific they insist on being, but also how evocative and almost sinister they cannot help but be:

Just look at it!
Give it up
Work it out
Put up with it
See it through
Stick at it
Stop it!
Here it comes
It had to happen
He was asking for it
Keep it in the family
Keep it dark
Cut it short
When you get down to it
It won't come to that

Would you believe it?
That's not the worst of it
I don't hold with it
I didn't mean it
Keep it quiet
Keep it to yourself
Word has it that . . .
Put it off
Put it on (play up, dramatize)
Put it out (disseminate information)
Put it about (be promiscuous)
It's no good
It's a shame
It won't do

Now, is it part of life, or is it rather the case that life – which is the rolling drama of human relationships mediated by ordinary language – must always use the it-idioms in order to defer or keep at bay everything that lurks and threatens to overthrow it? Does what we have come to call 'life' *have* to constitute itself by excluding it-all?

Here we recall a contrast that we have already made between the world-view of classical tragedy, and the world-view of the most important genre of postmodern popular drama, the soap opera.

In classical tragedy there is a presumption that it is, or ought to be, excludable from life. The royal, noble or heroic human being ought not to have to suffer incomprehensible torments and contradictions; and he certainly ought *not* to be brought down and ruined by it. But the protagonist has perhaps unwittingly offended the unknown Powers that be; or perhaps he is a pawn caught up in a conflict between the unknown Powers? Whichever it be, he now finds himself ruined by Powers and for reasons of which he knows nothing.

Classical tragedy then ends with a bleak vision of the human condition, and with It triumphant; but it also harbours an optimistic expectation. The royal, noble or heroic individual ought to be able to live an ideal life which is never swamped and destroyed by **It**. When **It gets him down**, he stays down. He cannot **cope with It**.

In 12, above, we compared the world-view of classical tragedy with the world-view of our own contemporary ordinariness. They have indeed some things in common, for heroic humanism has indeed something in common with democratic humanism. Ordinary language likes to regard itself as existing for the sake of 'gossip' – human networking. It prefers for the present to veil the nonhuman behind it-idioms. The best world is an only-human world, with all those bad dreams and shadowy threats banished to the outer fringes of the social world.

But the ordinary person differs from the tragic hero. Because she or he is 'low', she doesn't just sit in the ruins when disaster strikes, and die complaining mightily. She starts making plans for reconstruction, thinking about where the next meal is going to come from, and telling herself that *life must go on*. She keeps determinedly cheerful **in spite of it all**.

I admire the low people, with their indestructible faith in life. And indeed, admiration for 'low' survivors is itself a postmodern and highly democratic attitude. In classical times they admired the tragic hero who died and would have considered mere survival too low for him. Now, we think differently. We are learning to love life, to accept **everything that it can throw at us,** and yet still go on. In one way and another, we learn **to accept it,** or **to cope with it,** or **to fight it,** or **to laugh at it.** We are not impressed by heroes. The courage to survive is better than the courage to die, because it honours life. And we should admire the low person's ability to **take it,** and keep coming back.

Postmodern religiousness, we are suggesting, is characterized by a determined attempt to familiarize it, and to accept it as part of life. As far as possible, we will try to assimilate it into the human world; and what cannot be assimilated will have to be regarded as a lingering bad dream.

25

We are the masters now

Postmodern popular culture, and especially the TV soap opera, is a low and plebeian celebration of life. It is endless, and indefinitely capacious. Like life itself, the soap-opera form is a large string bag, stretchy and shapeless enough to accommodate anything and everything.[27] It happily gobbles up both comedy and tragedy and actively *relishes* conflict, crime, suffering and death. The choice of the word 'opera' was well judged, because people do love to make an operatic performance out of the ordinary events of their lives. *That's the story of my life!*, people say with pleasure and recognition, because we all want narrative meaning in our lives, and we all want to achieve full self-expression. Why not? And from the ease with which soaps conjoin comedy and tragedy we learn how easy and good it is **to accept it** as being simply *part of life*.

All this means that postmodern culture cuts right across Nietzsche's celebrated distinction between master and slave moralities. Nowadays it is the *upper* classes who are relatively the more controlled and self-effacing, whereas popular culture is likely to be the more loud, dandified and life-affirming. It is indeed true that our postmodernity is 'low', plebeian and democratic in a way that derives from the Jewish and Christian traditions. But it is also the case that the very same postmodern culture can be solar and flamboyantly aestheticist. Consider, for example, the line that runs from Francis Bacon through Gilbert and George and on to Damien Hirst and the Britpop group. This tradition is assertively populist, swaggering, death-obsessed and nihilistic in a way that cuts across Nietzsche's scheme of thought. Today's disdainful aristocrat is more likely to be a professional sportsman or popstar than a Guards officer. The new mass culture may be highly populist, but it is not in the least inhibited, life-denying or slavish. Quite the opposite.

In this new cultural world ordinary people honour life by their determination *to keep going* and *to fight back*. They know now how to get organized, and how to campaign. They are very ready to air all their problems in public, and to **accept it** as part of life.

In all this they differ from the old heroic ethics. The hero sought **to rise above it all**, and to live by his own conception of his own honour. He loved the thought of an honourable death, and would certainly prefer to die rather than **let it get him down**. But our postmodern democratic populism has no use for greatness or for honour. Highly life-affirming, it sees no point at all in the idea of seeking an honourable death. Where's the attraction? He who is dead with honour is just as dead as he who has died dishonourably. High-flown language on war memorials now fills us not with pride, but with an overwhelming sense of sadness and futility. What a waste – and was not the old Jewish preacher right to honour life by saying:

> . . . but he who is joined to all the living has hope, for a living dog is better than a dead lion. For the living know that they will die, but the dead know nothing . . .[28]

In short, the values described by Nietzsche have been 'transvalued'. It is now the plebeian morality, the soap-opera morality, that most successfully loves life and says Yes to life. For what is healthy and life-affirming about fox-hunting and military exploits? Surely the true affirmer of life is not the honourably but very messily dead officer, but the plebeian survivor who, because he **always accepted it**, now always **somehow manages to get away with it**.

The aristocratic officer died because he couldn't accept **it** as having any part in him. **It** was too 'low' and humiliating for him to be able to **deal with it**. He scorned **it**. His pride forbade him any truck with **it**. So he died. But the plebeian, having no pride or honour, can afford to be patient and enduring. **He accepts it as part of life**, and so he survives.

Thus far, then, we entirely concur with the postmodern popular morality of the soap opera: we concur both with its view of life and with its view of it. The common people have always been **closer to it** – that is, closer to necessity, limitation, conflict, suffering and death. And because they are **closer to it**, they **understand it** better, and so can **get away with it**.

We have already noted the contrast between the conversation of the rich and the conversation of the poor. The conversation of the rich at social occasions sedulously avoids any mention of **it**, whereas the conversation of the poor positively relishes serious illness, gory surgery and a good cry at the funeral. The rich try to exclude **it** from consciousness and from polite society and, in the extreme case of an upper-class ethic, the truest nobleman lives only for his honour and tries to **cut it dead**. He scorns any acknowledgement of or compromise with **it**. He'd rather die – and he does. But the poor **just love it**. They'd better: they live so much closer to **it**. But they are the survivors, and there is no better way of demonstrating your commitment to life than to be a survivor.

I have lived in both worlds in my time, and I prefer the values of the poor and the soap operas. But how much further are we willing to go along these lines? In the plebeian Judeo-Christian morality, **it** is accepted as the Will of God. More, **it** may be given a human face, as God. So, while we have Nietzsche in mind, we may well ask ourselves whether, in popular Christianity, God is not the ultimate plebeian myth? Until as recently as the 1950s people were exhorted to see, and some of them *did* see, in the terminal illness that was slowly killing them the face of a loving Heavenly Father. At the time of writing it is still possible to hear people say, in connection with the sudden violent death of a group of much-loved young people, that 'God took the best for himself'. Concerning the same event, however, someone who refuses to go that far may be heard to say instead that **it makes you sick doesn't it?** He says into thin air: **I ask you: Life's a pig, innit?**

We are talking here about the familiar disagreement between theist and atheist – but we are seeing it in a new way, as being a *domestic* disagreement that arises *within* the postmodern popular morality that seeks to affirm life and **to accept it all.** How far can this **acceptance of it** go? Are we willing to personify **it** as God, and accept its cruelty as being *tough love?* Or do we say no, and **fight it?** Which answer does ordinary language now give?

This question arose earlier, in section 8, above. I repeat the answer that was given then: historically, the major religious traditions *often* personified **it** as God or a god, and *always* recommended submission to **it.** But in the past half-century the idioms that urge us to **fight it** have grown steadily more numerous and stronger. Ordinary language does not suddenly decide these issues one way or the other, but there is no doubt about which way the wind is blowing. The **fight-it** policy makes more sense, and at least sometimes pays off.

Even the Christian belief that passes for 'orthodox' has already accepted the point. For believers who say that when disaster strikes they turn for comfort to a loving God are very often careful to say that they do *not* now think of God as having directly *caused* the plane crash or the cancer. God can be found *in* the cancer, but we shouldn't think that God has directly *sent* the cancer.[29] They thus show that they have abandoned realistic theism (though they would doubtless deny it), and they leave themselves room for **fighting it** so as to ensure if possible **that such a thing never happens again.**

A complex religious shift has taken place: postmodern religious faith takes the **it**-element out of God, understanding God as a pure spiritual ideal of love, acceptance and forgiveness. The **it**-element that 'causes cancer' is taken into the human realm where it can be fought, understood, managed, conquered, assimilated. The final outcome of this process is a purely spiritual (**it**-less, or non-realist) idea of God in a purely human world.

26

Life, It and God

In the life-book we argued that in recent generations the old vocabulary and attitudes that used to surround God and faith in God have come instead to be refocussed about **life**. In effect, **life**, just the contingent flux of human social existence that animates us and in which we live and move and have our being, has become the religious object. Eternal life is now a way of living and experiencing just *this* life, and indeed a surprising amount of religious vocabulary has already been reassigned to this-worldly duties. Many words such as revelation, miracle, grace, ecstasy, icon, and charisma are now familiar to everyone in their new extended senses, while their original theological use is forgotten. Religion is now not so much a way of cultivating the hope of another and better life, as rather a way of intensifying the manner in which we live and experience *this* life.

As the **Id** in Freudian psychology is the dark, and largely-hidden side of the self, so **It** is the dark, and mysterious side of life that we would prefer not to be reminded of just now, thank you very much.

What then is the relationship between **It** and God? If God is now very largely brought down into life and our experience of life; and if **It** is **life**'s shadow-side or Other, then has **It** in effect now become God's and our cosmic Adversary – or in Hebrew, *Satan*?

The story is complicated, and the point at issue is one upon which ordinary language is perhaps wisely non-committal. As we indicated earlier, ordinariness is much less moralistic and certainly much less dualistic than orthodoxy; and in any case, orthodoxy itself has strong and confusing internal countercurrents. After all, in the developed Christian world-picture Christ is the supreme cosmic Judge and Satan the cosmic prison governor – and 'Lucifer' is a traditional title of *both*. They both serve the one and the same great divine Purpose, and it is not surprising that *in their heavenly aspect* they look so much alike. They are both sons of God: the one is God's eternal and only begotten Son, and the other is the first of the created Sons of God. And it follows from the Divine Omnipotence that God, as First Cause of everything, is the cause of evil as well as good; and Hell is as much a place where God's will is done as Heaven is.

That God's will is done in Hell is an idea familiar to readers of Dante,[30] though sometimes shocking to modern Christians, who may be unaware of how much the idea of God has changed in the modern period. That God sends evil as well as good is an idea familiar to readers of the Bible:

Does evil befall a city,
        unless the Lord has done it?

I gave you cleanness of teeth in all your cities,
        and lack of bread in all your places . . .

And I also withheld the rain from you
        when there were yet three months to the harvest;
I would send rain upon one city,
        and send no rain upon another city;
one field would be rained upon,
        and the field on which it did not rain withered . . .

I smote you with blight and mildew . . .

I sent among you a pestilence after the manner of Egypt;
        I slew your young men with the sword . . .[31]

Indeed, one may fairly say that in the most robust classical monotheism, in the Hebrew Bible, in the Qu'ran, and right up to Calvin, God was just It, both for good and ill. God caused all things and ruled all things. Satan and his cohorts in their kingdom of Hell were in no sense a *rival* empire that opposed God's universal realm; on the contrary, they were just a department of it. But with the Enlightenment – that is, from the early seventeenth century – the movement towards a purely ethical or 'non-realistic' understanding of God began. Increasingly, God was associated not with Everything, but with ideal goodness and love only. Satan fell into a decline. A new branch of theology, 'theodicy', set out to show that God's government of the cosmos is *unmixedly* wise and good. All is for the best. There *is* no It, no shadow-side. Whatever is, is right.

What do we make then of the return of It in common speech, as Enlightenment optimism fades from about the 1870s, and the much darker world-view of the twentieth century takes shape? From now on, the object of religious love and commitment is increasingly going to be **life**: that is, the human world, human values, art. The old religious vocabulary will increasingly be reshaped so as to function *only within* the human life-world.

As for whatever may be thought to surround and to bear down upon the human life-world, well, our language does everywhere bear indirect witness to it. The crucial point is that we have lost every form of the old 'theological' and comforting belief in a pre-established harmony, a ready-made fit, between ourselves and the extrahuman world. We no longer suppose that *our own language* was already being spoken by Spirit-beings before ever we existed, as happens in Genesis 1. We were not specially made to fit into the extrahuman world, and the extrahuman world was not specially made to be a comfortable home for us. Our language is simply and solely *our* language, and our human life-world is the only world it builds or knows. Nothing guarantees any special relationship between our language and the shape of the extrahuman, and we have no knowledge that the extrahuman is either interested in us or intelligible to us. Furthermore, nothing whatever assures us that the extrahuman **it** in any way echoes or endorses our values. *We* are the only makers of our language, our values, our creeds and our social structures. We are at home in the friendly human life-world, because we evolved it, and have made it to be our home. We made all the rules, and the pictures on the walls are pictures of our gods. We built the walls: we painted the pictures. But there is no guarantee whatever that our rules, our furniture, or our images somehow copy or reflect the shape of a larger cosmic Home beyond our human home in our own human life-world. Inevitably, then, with the decline of the old optimistic theological realism our **it-talk** has returned and expanded along with our growing sense of cosmic homelessness. Whatever surrounds us is in no way akin to us.

We can now attempt a final characterization of the It-talk in ordinary language, and what it is telling us. We begin with, and then we develop and enlarge a little, the sketch given earlier in section 15 (pp.58f.).

1. We are the only beings who live in a very large and complex language-formed world of our own making.

2. The basic world is this our human life-world.

3. Life is the process of things in the human life-world.

4. Ordinary language is the principal and basic currency of the human life-world.

5. Ordinary language is very largely – and almost entirely – phatic; that is, it is chiefly used, not to describe facts but to express feelings, and for purposes of social interaction. Our utterances are speech-acts, moves in various 'situations' or language-games.

6. The human world does not consist solely of a web or net of communication, with messages flying back and forth. For the content of the messages *itself* attests the presence and the constraining influence of an extrahuman **It**, a background that is pervasive and impersonal – or at least, ungendered.

7. Being outside the human life-world, **it** cannot be talked about directly. It is often therefore seen as the unmentionable, the unspeakable, the unnameable, the unavowable, the indescribable and the ineffable. We may be reluctant, unable or forbidden to specify it in any more detail.

8. Our it-idioms suggest that we see much of human life as a struggle to keep **it** at bay or under control, and thereby to maintain the integrity of the human world.

9. Our it-idioms, and the feelings associated with them,

suggest that we are still troubled by bad dreams; by many ancient ideas about Fate, Destiny, Necessity and the Will of God; about Luck, Chance and Fortune; about monsters and supernatural enemies; and about death, darkness and nothingness. So are we battling against real foes – or only against our own ancient bad dreams? Ordinary language doesn't say.

* * *

That is as far as ordinary language can take us. So far as it is concerned, we know only that we are still troubled by ancient thoughts of various extrahuman beings, pressures and threats. Might we one day **forget it**, and come to see the human world as simply outsideless? We might – but ordinary language does not say so.

And am I right to say that we should forget the traditional association between God and **It**, and should see all our religious ideas as relating only to the human life-world? I might be – but ordinary language doesn't say so. Ordinary language prefers to keep its options open for the present, and it may be wise to do so.

My own view, argued elsewhere, is that **it** is on the way out. In depth-psychology there used to be a slogan running 'Where Id was, there Ego shall be'. Paraphrasing, we might say: 'Where **It** was, there the human realm will be'. At least some of **it** – life's sheer contingency, for example – we are already learning to accept as part of our own human world. Some more of **it** we'll fight and assimilate and accept. Eventually, only the old bad dreams will remain, and they can be allowed slowly to fade. In ways that William Blake, for example, has indicated, Christianity's future is to become the first radical humanist religion. The word, the flesh, and the human world: that is all there is, and it is enough for us. But this is a minority view. Ordinary language is smart, but it is also eclectic, and cautious. It will not yet quite go all the way with me, alas. But one day it will, I hope.

27

What does it all mean?

What is it all about?, **What is it all in aid of?**, **What's the point of it all?**, **What does it all add up to?** Questions such as these seek to totalize it as **it all**, and then ask for some kind of *pattern* in **it all**, some kind of myth or narrative about **where it's all going** and **what purpose it all serves**. People are asking for some sort of extrahuman and ready-made **meaning of it all**. In short, they are asking for objective theism and for the whole Plan of Salvation from the Creation of the World to the Last Judgement; or alternatively they might be persuaded to accept some other similar story that can serve as a satisfactory replacement for it.

Ordinary language does include much that makes this demand. But we have seen that the it-idioms that it gives us are too varied to be totalizable – or perhaps it would be better to say simply that nothing assures us that all of **it** can be taken up into a single great totality. And indeed the discussion in 9, above, (pp.34ff.) suggested that we use the expression **it all** to *express* cosmic feeling, rather than to *describe* a cosmic totality. In which case whatever unifies **it all** and makes sense of **it all** must be sought *in ourselves* rather than out there.

Ordinary language recognizes this, too; for as well as the idioms that demand unity, pattern and purpose out there, we also find in language many non-realist idioms that clearly acknowledge that it is we ourselves who must labour, whether successfully or not, to impose unity, order and purpose upon experience:

What do you make of it all?
Can you make any sense of it?

I can just make it out . . .
It means nothing to me
I can't make anything of it
I don't get it / It escapes me / I can't see it
It beats me (= it eludes me)
I can make nothing of it
What's the point? (. . . of anything, of it all)

And we may add in here the little group of relativistic it-depends idioms mentioned earlier:

That depends
It depends on what you mean by . . .
It all depends
It depends on how you look at it

Realists often claim that it is obvious that their view is the view of common sense, and that they occupy the high ground. But ordinary language says otherwise: the idioms just quoted show that **making sense of it all** is a very difficult and uncertain business. **The meaning of it all** is not antecedently laid on for us; rather, it is something we must strive to *make out*, or to project as an ethical possibility:

I can see possibilities in it
I don't know what she sees in him / She must feel she
can make something of him

'Seeing meaning' is often a matter of seeing future possible improvements that one may be able to make, and thereby perhaps bring about a state of affairs that will **make it all worthwhile**.

Ordinary language does not decide clearly and unambiguously between realism and non-realism. But in the matter of **seeing meaning in it all** our language casts at least as many votes for the non-realist point of view as for the other.

From the non-realist point of view talk about the need to find **meaning in it all** expresses a 'cosmic' emotional response, an imaginative vision of how **things** might be otherwise, and perhaps commitment to an ethical task. And ordinary language has plenty in it to support such a view.

28

Democratizing religious thought

If you agree with me in holding the typically anti-realist (and, of course, blindingly obvious) view that it is we human beings who have ourselves collectively and over the millennia evolved all our languages and knowledge-systems, and that we humans are ourselves the makers of all our meanings, truths and values; and if therefore you also acknowledge that we are *of course* the only makers of all our religions and philosophies and world-views, then surely you will agree with me that we ought to start treating questions in philosophy, theology and ethics in a more democratic way than has been usual hitherto? Humankind's immemorial collective creativity is so great that it has evolved the whole world of human language and thought, including not only the whole of natural science, but also the whole of religion, philosophy and ethics. Surely we should give due credit to the communal creativity that has made us what we are and has given to us all our powers, and we should give up the notion that the highest kind of truth can come to us only through specially gifted and inspired people, and from a Source quite outside the common run of humanity?

Hitherto, philosophy and theology have been plagued respectively by extreme élitism and by authoritarianism. The great philosophers have been seen as geniuses whose teachings were developed quite independently of the common mind of ordinary people; and the great religious innovators (especially in the 'Abrahamic' group of faiths) have been seen as inspired prophets, conveying to us authoritative teachings quite beyond the grasp of our ordinary faculties. These traditional ideas are obviously erroneous, because every great philosopher inherited a vocabulary, had a teacher, and studied his predecessors; and similarly, every 'inspired prophet' appeared in a particular cultural context and communicated his message in an already-extant *human* vocabulary. *And it could not have been otherwise.* There is no absolute innovator, and those who seemed to their contemporaries to be the most shockingly innovative are recognized by posterity as having said things that were just sitting there waiting to be said. The most familiar illustration of the point is the case of Charles Darwin, who created one of the most important and powerful theories ever put forward by anyone, merely by joining up a number of ideas that were commonplace in his time.

So we should forget élitist and supernaturalist ideas about Reason and Truth. Instead we should investigate the metaphysics of ordinariness; we should examine the popular wisdom of life that is conveyed in the idiomatic phrases of our common language; and in the manner of Tolstoy and Wittgenstein we should regard ordinariness with intellectual respect as being the substrate – the soil out of which everything grows, and into which everything in the end returns. Ordinary language stands alone. It is not subject to any external regulator that has authority to assess it and tell it how to correct itself. As Wittgenstein said: 'This language-game is played!' – and that is that. So ordinary language is just current, and that's all. The process by which it has evolved has ensured that it works: its currency and its working are the same thing. (Notice here that you cannot even imagine coming across a human community whose language *doesn't* work.) So ordinary language is current, it works, **it is what it is,** and that's that. And it also incorporates a large and fairly loose-textured body of philosophical, religious and moral wisdom which (as I have been trying to show) is rather more coherent and interesting than it gets credit for.

I am arguing, then, that if we are to make any progress in religious thought, we should begin by studying the philosophy of life and the religious and moral ideas that belong to us because they are built into our language. They are *data*: they are current, which means that they work. They are part of our common view of the world and valuation of life. And I am also suggesting a new discipline and test of truth. Everyone who writes or teaches in the areas of philosophy, theology and ethics develops an itch to criticize ordinariness, tidy it up, and elaborate a personal system of 'over-beliefs' (*Uberglaube*). It is then claimed that the individually-produced work of systematic philosophy, theology or ethics is a great *improvement* upon the popular wisdom of life. The presumption here is that ordinary people, with nothing but ordinary language to go by, are floundering in a state of mental confusion. They are lost sheep, in great need of a shepherd-teacher who will tell them with authority what to believe and how they should live. But my argument, here and in the life-book, has been that the vision of the human condition which is embodied in ordinary language is more substantial and even *formidable* than we have supposed. It evolves historically, and it rests upon the very widest consensus. What is more, it manifestly *works*. We should ask ourselves whether our special creeds and systems of thought really do much better, in *practice*, than ordinary language – and I suggest that in the majority of cases the answer is humbling.

In these two little books about **Life** and about **It** and **It-All**, I have tried to show that the vision of the human condition embodied in our current idiomatic speech is interesting, and that by attending to the ways in which it is *changing* we can learn some important lessons about the way the wind is blowing. In particular:

1. The religious object, the focus of religious attention, is now beyond doubt coming to be purely immanent within the human life-world. It is simply a fact that in everyday speech God-talk has become very impoverished. Talk about a heavenly world beyond death is, if anything, even weaker. Almost nothing of interest has been added to it for a very long time, whereas Life-talk, already very rich, is still growing. Life *itself* – the word being used in new ways – has already become the ordinary person's religious object. It is a non-realist religious object, of course, because life is not a substance and has no objective reality over and above what we are doing within it and making

of it. But the religion of life is a real religion. One is, so to say, passionately committed to **the living of life**, and to **loving life**. **The feeling of being alive** (*Lebensgefühl*) takes the place of the old sense of being filled with the divine Spirit.

2. By its very nature as the human communication-system, ordinary language posits, or aspires after, the world-view of radical humanism. It is Blakean. Reality consists of a society of human persons in converse with each other, and thereby managing their social relations, strengthening their social bonds and harmonizing their feelings about things. This vision of a purely-human world, in its most explicit form, derives from Jewish messianism and Christian millenarianism, and some of us still hope that Christianity may one day become *the* radical-humanist religion. Being what it is, ordinary language *must* posit the world-view of radical humanism – exactly the world-view which is also posited by the utopian strand in the Judaeo-Christian tradition.

3. Meanwhile, however, ordinary language is still troubled by bad dreams. By that, I mean that although in many social situations we **set it aside**, and talk as if nothing exists but ourselves, the *communio sanctorum*, the fellowship of the saints, our language still shows itself uncomfortably aware of the extra-human and encircling realm of it. Some of it fits peacefully into the human world; but other aspects of it seem profoundly threatening to us. If **it all** is only a bad dream, a residue left over from our past, we may hope that in time it will finally cease to threaten us. But ordinary language does not know the answer for sure. Perhaps **it all** will always trouble us in one or another of its many guises, as Necessity, Fate, Destiny, God, Fortune, Chance, Nothingness, Death or whatever? The jury is still out.

4. Ordinary language is not only phatic (concerned with bringing about or facilitating social interaction), but it is also rather strongly *emotivist*, and perhaps is currently becoming even more so. We speak in order to commune with others, expressing our own feelings, probing their feelings about things, and cautiously manoeuvring their and our feelings into line with each other. The human world is held together, not chiefly by the

Law, nor by contracts, nor by a shared body of knowledge, but by common feeling.

A young person who specializes in being extremely sociable and up-to-date has kindly supplied me with what I am assured are a collection of very recent it-idioms. They are markedly emotivist, including such phrases as **getting off on it**, used not in a chiefly sexual sense, but of enjoying something generally; **getting down on it**, again not primarily sexual,, but used rather of getting into the rhythm of something; **Can you feel it?**, meaning *do you dig it, do you respond to it*; **mad for it**, in the sense of simply liking it; and **Are you up for it?**, meaning, are you with us, and will you join us.[32]

Idioms such as these are a world away from Platonism, with its high valuation of knowledge and theoretical understanding. They are also a world away from the scientific attitude, which indeed has as yet had rather little effect upon ordinary language. These idioms are Lawrentian, emotivist. They are interested in life and gut-feeling. And if ordinary language tells us anything, it is that *that* interest comes first.

To democratize religious thought, I am saying, we need to take more seriously the way ordinary language views *and must view* the world, and also the ways in which it is changing. Ordinary language now incorporates a religion of Life and feeling, purely immanent and non-realist, that one might regard as a biologized version of religious existentialism. Ordinary language, being what it is, posits *and must posit* the world-view of radical humanism, which is closely related to the old utopian strain in Judaeo-Christianity.[33] Ordinary language recognizes that much of what we call it can without great difficulty be smoothly incorporated into the human life-world. But when we totalize **it all**, our language still shows us to be troubled by bad dreams of a larger non-human and deeply Alien backdrop, encircling the warm and brightly-lit human world. Some will still want to locate the Sacred in **It Out There**. Ordinary language is wary about that, and for the most part tells us to put our whole trust just in Life and the human lifeworld.

That's the way it is. If there is to be serious religious thought in the future, I suggest that it must start from, and perhaps build upon and develop further, the world-view of ordinary language and our common experience as I have tried to describe it. If on the contrary you wish to develop a world-view and a style of religious thought that repudiates and breaks with ordinariness, I suggest that you have a lot of explaining to do. Is it really *possible* sanely to break with the world-view that is built into our language and therefore is constitutive of our very being? **I've told it like it is:** *am I wrong? Tell me!*

Index of Idioms

This list of about 450 items contains the **it** and **it all** idioms cited in the text, together with a few **things** and **everything** idioms. There are also lists of **take it** idioms on p.61, above, and **God** idioms on p.50.

A
What's it all about?
Say no more about it
The absolute It
Accepting it
Accept it as the will of God
What does it all add up to? / It doesn't add up
What is it all in aid of?
It's all I can do (to do something)
It's as much as I can do (to do something)
It ain't necessarily so
You can't argue with it
Amen to that
I don't see anything in it
Reporting it as it happens
Telling it as it is
As it was
Everything has been left just as it was
Asking for it
As you like it
What it all amounts to
At it again
At it like knives

Avowing it
I need to get away from it all

B
It is not as bad as all that
He's got it bad (for her)
I can't bear it
It beats me
It ill becomes him to do that
I can't believe it
I don't believe it
Would you believe it?
Perhaps it has all been for the best
Make the best of it
Maybe it has been a blessing in disguise
It seems better to . . .
It were better for him that he had never been born
It's a breeze
It's beyond me
Not a bit of it
Get it down in black and white
Blast it!
Blow it!
Bringing it out into the open
There ought to be a book about it
It's a boy!
Bursting with it
Busily at it

C
It came to pass
It is the case that . . .
It will catch up with you one day
Cheat it (take a questionable short cut. For the indefinite
    object here, Compare Walk it, Lord it over . . . Queen it,
    etc.)
The cheek of it

There's no choice about it
Closer to it
It is cold
Come to terms with it
How comes it that . . .?
If it comes to it
He had it coming to him
Come off it
It won't come to that
It is idle to complain
She does not conceal it
It doesn't count
It had crossed my mind
Cut it down to size
Cut it dead
Cut it out
Cut it short

D
God damn it all!
It's too dangerous
Keep it dark
It's all in a day's work
Dealing with it
It all depends
It depends on how you look at it
It's a disgrace
There's not a lot I can do about it
It's dogged as does it
Do it now
It doesn't do to do that
I don't get it
It won't do
I don't know how you do it
It shouldn't happen to a dog
Now you've done it
I don't doubt it

It's down to me
When you get down to it
Get down on it (= get into the rhythm of it)
It's a dream
Drop it!
Dying for it

E
Take it easy
Take things easy
Where will it all end?
That's the end of it
It's not the end of the world
Enjoy it; make the most of it while it lasts
It escapes me
To establish it
Is everything all right?
The man who has everything
That's exactly it
Put it down to experience

F
On the face of it
Face up to it
It's not fair
Can you feel it?(= do you dig it, do you enjoy it?)
Fight it / Fight it to the end / Fight it all the way / Fight back
    at it
It figures
Finding it hard to cope with
It all frightens me
If you've got it, flaunt it
Forget it
You're full of it
It's a funny old world

G
It's only a game
Get at it / Get to it! / Get on to it / Get off on it (= enjoy it)
Get it (understand)
Get it done, Get it on / Getting it on (= having sex)
Getting around to it
Getting away from it all
Get on with it? / Get with it! / Get it right
Don't let it get you down
When you get down to it
It's getting on top of me
Getting around to it
He'll never get away with it
You'll get over it
There's no getting away from it
The It-girl
It's a girl!
The gist of it
Go it alone
Go it blind (= double the ante without looking at the cards)
Go for it! Get to it!
Got it! (= I've found the answer)
Go through with it
He's no longer got it (= he's lost his touch)
God's got it in for me
    (God-idioms are listed on p.39)
So it goes
He's got what it takes
It's all going very well
I can't go on with it
As good as it gets
Grin and bear it

H
I've had it
It had to be / It had to happen
At it hammer and tongs

You haven't seen the half of it yet
It can't happen here / It happens / As it happens
Make sure that it never happens again
Hard at it
It's a hard life
That hardly comes into it
The man who has it all
Just hating it
He thinks he's it
I can't help it
It can't be helped
Here it is / Here it comes
I don't hold with it / I don't hold it against you
It's hopeless
It's all going horribly wrong
It is hot
How are things with you? / How is it with you?
That's how it goes
How is it going? / How's it all going? / How goes it?
That's how it is
How it was in my day
Does it hurt? / It hurts

I
It all
Is it? / It is / Isn't it? / It can't be / It is so / So it is / It is what
    it is
It is fulfilled
It's hell
Am I just imagining it?
What it's up to
It's all up with me(= I've had it, I'm done for)
It's all over
It's an ill wind that blows nobody any good
It's best not to get too involved
It's going to be all right
It is idle to deny that . . .

It isn't what it was

J
It's more than my job's worth
It's no joke / It's serious
It's just as well
Do it justice
Just do it!

K
Keep it dark / Keep it quiet / Keep it in the family
Keep it up
I knew it!
It knocks you sideways
I don't know what it is

L
It's too late / It's later than you think
Laugh it off
Learn from it
Leave it alone
Leave it at that
Leave it be / Leave it to me
Leaving it unsaid
Let it be / Let it not be so
Let it out (of a secret)
What's it like?
It's just like him to have done that
Take life as it comes
The long and short of it
By the look/looks of it / It looks like it / Just look a
It looks good / It's looking good / That's the way
He's lost it
There's a lot of it about
There's not a lot you can do about it
It's love that makes the world go round
Loving it

If you don't like it then you must lump it
Like it or not

M
Mad for it (= liking it)
God made it so
I can't make any sense of it
Make it (success) / Make it clear / Make it plain / Make it up
Making light of it / Make the best of it / Make our peace
    with it
What do you make of it all? / I can't make anything of it
Make it out / Making sense of it all
It doesn't matter
May it not be so
What does it all mean?
Seeing meaning in it all / I didn't really mean it
Get the measure of it / Measure it up
Don't mention it!
It is as if it has a mind of its own
It's all in the mind
Don't miss it
There's a lot of money in it
It's only money
It's all too much / becoming a bit too much for me
There's not all that much to it
mystery to me
all

(of a bomb)
e to do . . .

It's no use
Having none of it
It was not to be / It just wasn't to be
There's nothing in it/to it / I can make nothing of it
It has come to my notice that
Best to say nowt about it

O
It has often occurred to me
Get it over and done with
Getting over it
It only shows
It leaves us no options/with no option

P
Pack it in!
Get it into perspective
You'll soon pick it up (learn the ropes, become familiar
     with it)
Life's a pig, isn't it?
Play it by ear
I can't see any point in it
What's the point of it all?
I thought it pointless to protest
I can see possibilities in it
Well, can you see any purpose behind it all?
Push it to the limit
Put it about (= be promiscuous)
You'll just have to put up with it
Put it across (= communicate successfully)
Put it down on paper
Put it off
Put it on (= show off, etc.)
Putting it on (pretending)
Put it out (= disseminate information)

Q
It's a question of . . .
It's really quite something

R
It is raining / It never rains but it pours
Read all about it
Be reconciled to it
Redeeming it all
It remains to be seen
It's going to be all right / Maybe it'll all come out right in the
    end
Resign yourself to it
It's all right
Get rid of it
Rise above it all
Rolling in it
Rubbing it in / rubbing his nose in it
Don't run away from it
Run for it!

S
There! I've said it / You've said it
I can't see it (= I don't understand)
See it through
See to it
It seems so / to be so
I don't know what she sees in him
Can you make any sense of it?
It's a shame
Shrug it off!
It make you sick, doesn't it?
It's as simple as that
Sit it out
It wasn't as straightforward as that
That's about the size of it
It's a small world

It's snowing
So be it
Sort it out / Sort it
By the sound of it
In spite of it all/everything
Let it stand / I can't stand it
Stick it out / Stick at it
Stop it
It strikes me that . . .

T
Tackle it head on
I don't want to talk about it
Take it (= suffer punishment etc.) / I can't take any more of
   it
   ' (Take-it idioms are listed on page 61)
Take it all in (understand everything)
You can't take it with you
Take life as it comes
Talking it over / Talking about it
Tell it like it is
That about wraps it up for now
That's about it for now
That's it / Is that it? / Was that it? / Is that all there is to it?
This is it
The thing in-itself
I'm on top of it / Things are getting on top of me
There isn't a thing we can do about it
There it is / There you have it
How are things with you?
Is this it? / This is it / How long can it go on like this?
I never give it a thought
Threw it all away
It's tough
The tragedy of it
Everything that it can throw at us
Turning against it / Maybe it'll all turn out right in the end

It takes two to tango
There are no two ways about it

U
It's best left unsaid / Leaving it unsaid
Up against it
Are you up for it? (= willing to join in)
Is he up to it?
Use it or lose it

W
Walking it
Maybe it just wasn't to be
Watch it!
The way of it / That's the way it is / Have it your own way
You can't have it both ways
Whatever it is / What is it? / What's it all about / What it is
You do your best, and where does it get you?
Where it's at
Think well of it
With it (= in tune, in the fashion)
It's no wonder that . . . / Makes you wonder though, doesn't
    it?
Word has it that . . .
Work it out
It could be worse / That's the worst of it / The worst of it is
    over now
I ask you, is it worth it?
Making it all worthwhile
It is written
It's all going pear-shaped/horribly wrong

Y
Oh yes, it is!
It could be you
It's all yours / You're it
Keep it to yourself

Notes

Introduction

1. *The New Religion of Life in Everyday Speech*, London: SCM Press 1999.
2. But see his *On Certainty*, Oxford: Basil Blackwell 1969, for example nos. 208, 209, 336.

Section 1

3. See *Halliwell's Film and Video Guide 1999*, ed. John Walker, New York: Harper Collins 1998, for details of other films whose titles begin with **Thing** or **It**. The 'Its' are a motley crew: the original *It* (1927), with Clara Bow, was a film about sex-appeal, a theme continued in such titles as *It Started In Paradise* (1952), *It Started With A Kiss* (1959), and *It Started With Eve* (1941). It-monster films include *It Came From Beneath the Sea* (1955), *It Came From Outer Space* (1953), *It Conquered The World* (1956), *It Lives Again* (1978), and *It! The Terror From Beyond Space* (1958). *It* is a mystery in such films as *It Could Happen to You* (1939) and *It Happened Tomorrow* (1945). The remaining twenty nine *It*-films are all feelgood romantic comedies – long the most popular film genre. Here the word *It* functions to provoke curiosity and get us into the mood for a pleasurable fantasy.
4. However, Mark C. Taylor has written a not-book: *Nots*, Chicago: the University of Chicago Press 1993. The word **not** has always had rich theological overtones, but **it** has developed them, for the most part, only recently – perhaps as elements of traditional supernatural belief have been consigned to the realm of **it**.

Section 4

5. See my *The Religion of Being* and *The Revelation of Being*, both London: SCM Press 1998.
6. See the life-book, cited above, Introduction, n.1.
7. Iris Murdoch's novel *The Time of the Angels* (1967) introduced the

idea that the Death of God – that is, the end of metaphysical realism, the breakdown of the central authority out there that used to hold everything together – is followed by a time of acute spiritual disorder in which undisciplined spirit-powers rampage through the world. I now disagree: perhaps the death of God is followed by a gradual sacralization of the whole life-world, and perhaps the decline of the authority of Holy Writ is followed by a certain sacralization of Writing generally. In *The Revelation of Being* I similarly indicated that we may be able to see the way the whole contingent world presents itself as a secularization of God.

Section 5

8. Luther Link, *The Devil: A Mask without a Face*, London: Reaktion Books 1995.

9. Georges Bataille, *Eroticism*, tr. Mary Dalwood, French 1957; ET London: Calder and Boyars 1962, repr. Marion Boyars 1987, 1990.

10. E.g., Psalms 16.6, 78.55.

Section 6

11. Geoffrey Parrinder, *African Mythology*, London: Paul Hamlyn 1967, p.19. Parrinder's discussion prompts one to think that *pre*-philosophical African talk about God sounds much the same as *post*-philosophical talk of God in the West.

12. Anthony Burgess, *The End of the World News*, 1982.

Section 7

13. *The New Religion of Life*, p.27.

14. And James himself cheerfully admitted it: see *The Will to Believe and Other Essays in Popular Philosophy* (1896), the first three essays, and especially 'The Sentiment of Rationality'.

Section 9

15. Note that 'making it up' may apply to a face, a quarrel, a shortfall or a story – an excellent example of our language's weird duplicity.

Section 10

16. René Passeron, *René Magritte*, tr. Elisabeth Abbot, New York: Filipacchi Books 1980, p.12.

Section 11

17. A stock phrase from the 18th century philosopher-bishop, Joseph Butler.

18. From the science-fiction novelist Kurt Vonnegut. See especially his *Slaughterhouse-Five*.

19. The first was the use of **it** to evoke the angry face of sex. See p.11, above.

Section 13

20. In the Introduction to *Three Weeks*.

Section 17

21. *As It Was* and *World Without End* are published together in a single volume, London: Faber and Faber 1956.

22. See his *Theodicy* (1710), tr. E.M. Huggard, London: Routledge 1952.

Section 19

23. For a more detailed and accurate account, see R. J. Brown, *English Farmhouses*, London: Robert Hale 1982, repr. 1983.

Section 22

24. See section 5, above.
25. Genesis 4.7, RSV.

Section 23

26. In Zen Buddhism the theme of finding, catching and taming the bull is a venerable metaphor for the spiritual life. See the *Ten Bulls* by Kakuan (China, twelfth century), in Paul Reps, *Zen Flesh, Zen Bones*, London: Penguin Books 1971; and Myokyo-ni, *Gentling the Bull*, London: the Zen Centre 1988. On Ch'an, Chinese Zen, there is now a very good book: Dale S. Wright, *Philosophical Meditations on Zen Buddhism*, Cambridge University Press 1998.

Section 25

27. I am indebted to Hugh Rayment-Pickard for pointing out to me the highly postmodern character of soap opera as a cultural form.
28. Ecclesiastes 9.4f.

29. See John A. T. Robinson's last sermon, 'Learning from Cancer' (23 October 1983); in *Where Three Ways Meet: Last Essays and Sermons*, London: SCM Press 1987, pp.189–194.

Section 26

30. *Inferno*, 3:1–9.
31. Amos 3.6b; 4.6a, 7, 9a, 10a.

Section 28

32. In fact, Jonathon Green's superb *Dictionary of Slang*, London: Cassell 1998 does record **get off on it**, and describes **up for it** as nineteenth century.

33. In his *Anxious Angels: A retrospective view of religious existentialism*, London: Macmillan 1999, pp.73f., George Pattison has a fascinating passage about Dostoyevsky's *A Raw Youth*, 1875. In the novel, Versiliev clearly foresees the emergence, after the death of God and the transition to a radical-humanist world, of the religion of life:

> . . . all the wealth of love lavished of old upon Him who was immortal, would be turned upon the whole of nature, on the world, on men, on every blade of grass. They would inevitably grow to love the earth and life as they gradually became aware of their own transitory and finite nature . . .

And even more astonishingly, Versiliev sees the religion of life as opening the way to a new epiphany of Christ.

Sources

Interesting it-idioms are not easy to find. I have consulted the principal Oxford reference books, including *The Oxford English Dictionary*, Second Edition of 1989, repr. with corrections 1991; *The New Oxford Dictionary of English*, ed. Judy Pearsall, 1998; the *Oxford Dictionary of English Idioms*, edd. A.P. Cowie, R. Mackin and I.R. McCaig, 1993; and the *Oxford Concise Dictionary of Proverbs*, 1982, reissued 1996.

For film and book titles, I have consulted *Halliwell's Film and Video Guide: 1999 Edition, Revised and Updated*, ed. John Walker, Harper Collins 1998; and (with the help of John Cupitt) the booklists offered on the Internet by Amazon.

For slang, there is the very large and illuminating *The Cassell Dictionary of Slang*, ed. Jonathon Green, London: Cassell 1998. Green's huge collection of it-idioms confirms a point I make in the text to the effect that it-idioms become more numerous, and also more scatological and sexual, the more colloquial and slangy language becomes. See for example his entry describing the slang uses of **It**, which begins: '1. [late 16C+] sexual intercourse. 2. [mid-19C+] the male or female genitals. 3. [late 19C] a chamberpot.' But Green yields plenty of highly interesting it-idioms, if one searches, for example, under *do, go, get it . . ., have it . . ., make it . . ., take it . . .,* and so on. At least one learns that sex generates more new language at a faster rate than any other human concern.

Another worthwhile source of (politer) it-idioms can be found in the big Collins two-language dictionaries, English/French : French/English and English German : German/ English. These dictionaries supply the language student with a repertoire of stock phrases, phrases so familiar to the native speaker that we might otherwise overlook them and fail to remark how curious they are.

And **that is about it**. Indeed, this little book was first written to the title **Read all about it!**, because there are so few places where one can do so. But I never really expected to get away with such a title.

Index of Names